Testing Student Achievements and Aptitudes

THE LIBRARY OF EDUCATION

A Project of The Center for Applied Research in Education, Inc.

G. R. Gottschalk, Director

Categories of Coverage

I	II	III
Curriculum and Teaching	Administration, Organization, and Finance	Psychology for Educators
IV	V	VI
History, Philosophy, and Social Foundations	Professional Skills	Educational Institutions

Testing Student Achievements and Aptitudes

J. STANLEY AHMANN

Professor of Psychological Research
Colorado State University

The Center for Applied Research in Education, Inc.
New York

Second Printing .... July, 1966

LIBRARY OF CONGRESS
CATALOG CARD NO.: 62–15494

PRINTED IN THE UNITED STATES OF AMERICA

Foreword

For many decades professional education has been capitalizing to a highly profitable degree on the theories and supporting research of the behavioral sciences, particularly in psychology, sociology, and cultural anthropology. In many respects the greatest contribution has come from psychology, especially that aspect of psychology which is devoted to the study of the uniqueness of each individual. This realm of individual differences was of great interest to researchers such as James McKeen Cattell who, at the end of the last century, studied individual variations in the nature and rapidity of reactions to various stimuli such as words, colors, and letters. From such humble beginnings has sprung widespread and intensive study of the nature and amount of the unique characteristics which each of us possesses.

The study of individual differences has contributed substantially to at least two important trends in the science of psychology. One of these is the increasing concern for the individual as a person facing a variety of problems in his day-to-day existence. A second major trend is the increasing attention given to the development of psychological tests and diagnostic techniques in the areas of achievement, aptitude, interest, and personal-social adjustment. Both of these trends are of great importance to the development of professional education.

It is fitting that one of the volumes of the Library of Education is devoted to the question of the use of psychological testing in education. As the title suggests, *Testing Student Achievements and Aptitudes* does not deal with the application of the entire range of psychological tests and diagnostic techniques in the classroom. Various types of measurements, including those in the area of personal-social adjustment, are not included. This volume is limited to a discussion of the ways in which psychological tests of achievement and aptitude can be used in education. This is indeed a major task.

The importance of the role of tests in teaching is obvious. Both achievement and aptitude tests provide information which is essential for the effective selection of learning situations and conditions which will capitalize on the student's previous development. Achievement tests are used to provide information for the evaluation of success in achieving selected educational objectives. Acceptable achievement and aptitude tests must be available and used appropriately. It is the purpose of this book to describe the principles on the basis of which such tests are built, to examine the methods of building them, to illustrate the proper use of them and the interpretation of the results yielded by them, and to appraise in general the utility of these instruments in the educational process.

This book has been written by Dr. J. Stanley Ahmann, Professor of Psychological Research and Assistant to the President of Colorado State University. He completed his doctoral studies at Iowa State University in 1951, following which he spent nine years at Cornell University as Professor of Educational Psychology in the Division of Educational Psychology of the School of Education. In addition to this publication, he has written a number of articles devoted to psychological testing, statistical methodology, and educational evaluation. He has co-authored three books: *Statistical Methods in Educational and Psychological Research, Evaluating Pupil Growth,* and *Evaluating Elementary School Pupils.* This background, plus numerous professional activities conducted in conjunction with teachers, counselors, and school administrators, provides the basis upon which this volume was written.

ERIC F. GARDNER
Professor of Education and Psychology
Syracuse University

Contents

CHAPTER I

Evaluating Student Achievement

Many years ago Lord Kelvin, the British mathematician and physicist, was reported to have said, "When you can measure what you are speaking about and express it in numbers, you know something about it." When Lord Kelvin made this statement, he probably was not addressing it to the area of psychology; yet, what he said with respect to mathematics and physics can also be said of the behavioral sciences. Moreover, even though he made the statement at the turn of the twentieth century, it is as true now as it was then.

What does Lord Kelvin's statement mean in terms of psychological testing and its impact on the schools and universities of today? At the very least, it means that those interested in professional education know only what their measuring instruments reveal when they seek to determine the individual differences present in students and the degree to which the behavioral patterns of these students change as a result of educational experiences. In other words, the degree to which we know and understand the educational process and its impact upon the student is determined to a large extent by the degree of reliability and validity of the psychological tests used in the educational process, that is, the degree of consistency of the test scores and the degree to which they serve the purposes intended.

It is well-known that the degree of reliability and validity of the psychological tests commonly used in education is much less than that typically present in the measuring instruments used in the physical and biological sciences. However, in many instances there exists a sufficient degree of reliability and validity to allow evaluations to be made of pupil changes in behavior and, ultimately, of the effectiveness of educational programs.

In psychological testing there is the problem of obtaining a realistic view of the usefulness of the tests as they can be applied in formal education. On the one hand, we cannot allow ourselves to be cynical with respect to the use of psychological tests because of their inaccuracies. The testing movement began in this century, and, in view of its youth, the progress has been amazing. On the other hand, we cannot allow ourselves to be overconfident about the utility of psychological tests in the classroom. Someplace between cynicism and overconfidence is a position of healthy skepticism which allows the student, his parents, his teachers, his counselors, and the administrators of his school to appreciate the value of psychological tests and yet not be overwhelmed by extreme statements, either positive or negative.

The Nature of Measurement

To understand the role of psychological tests in education today, it is well to examine the nature of the measuring process. Measurement, in general terms, is *the process of assigning symbols to observations in some meaningful and consistent manner*. The measurement process has at least four well-defined levels.[1] These levels are the nominal, ordinal, interval, and ratio levels.

Levels of measurement. The *nominal level* is sometimes called the classification level. This identification stems from the fact that the nominal level is nothing more than a set of mutually exclusive classes, each class being represented by a letter, name, or number. The members of each class resemble each other more in some particular respect than they resemble members of any other class. Thus, the nominal level of measurement possesses equivalence, for each class contains some degree of internal homogeneity.

There are numerous illustrations of the nominal level outside formal education. For instance, the postal zones assigned in a large city or the numbers given to automobile license plates are measurements of the nominal type. Job classifications such as teacher, counselor, and administrator, and student classifications such as male and female or honors group, normal group, and retarded group are also measurements of the nominal type.

The nominal type is the lowest level of measurement. The data accumulated in measurements of this type are sometimes called enumeration data. The number of entities which have fallen into a particular class have simply been counted, causing some people to

[1] Irving Lorge, "The Fundamental Nature of Measurement," in *Educational Measurement,* ed. E. F. Lindquist (Washington, D.C.: American Council on Education, 1951), pp. 533–59; and Sidney Siegel, "Nonparametric Statistics," *American Statistician,* 11 (June 1957), pp. 13–19.

wonder whether this type of numbering is measurement at all. True, it is much different from other levels of measurement, but, on the other hand, it does conform to the general definition of measurement which we are using. Bear in mind that the assigned symbols may be numbers, letters, or, in some instances, even geometric signs which at a glance seem to have little or no significance.

The *ordinal level* of measurement is commonly called the ranking level. This level is one step above the nominal level in that it is characterized not only by equivalence but also by order. The entities in the various classes stand in some kind of relationship to each other. The results of the "Miss America" beauty contest and the order of finish (win, show, and place) of a horse race are appropriate illustrations of this level of measurement. Another very common use of the ordinal level of measurement is the ranking of high school graduates in terms of their position within their graduating class. In the academic world we find the professorial classifications following the ordinal pattern. The full professor, the associate professor, the assistant professor, and the instructor are roughly classified in terms of prestige and, in many cases, in terms of salary.

Ordinal measurement is more common than nominal measurement in the identification of student traits. For instance, teachers will often identify the general physical health and the general emotional health of a student in terms of three, or possibly five, categories. For example, teachers might label a student's physical health as above average, average, or below average. Student achievement, particularly in the psychomotor area, is frequently ranked in terms of its superiority.

The third level of measurement is known as the *interval level.* Consistent with the pattern established by the nominal and ordinal levels, this level possesses the characteristics of the ordinal level plus a new characteristic known as *equality of intervals.* The phrase means that the distance or difference between any adjacent classes on the scale is known numerically and is the same for any pair of adjacent classes. Hence, there is a constant unit of measurement. The interval level of measurement is well illustrated by temperature readings as measured on the Fahrenheit and centigrade scales. In both cases, for a given system the amount of heat needed to increase the temperature of the system one degree is constant from each temperature reading to the next (if one ignores special problems at the melting and boiling of the substances involved).

Well-developed psychological tests which measure unitary psychological traits are thought to yield scores which are of the interval type. Equal changes in the score levels are considered to be equivalent to equal changes in the degree to which the trait is present. This statement is quite defensible when we consider the scores near the center of a distribution of scores, but it becomes less defensible when we consider the very low scores or very high scores at either end of the distribution.

The last level of measurement is the *ratio level.* It possesses the three characteristics of the interval level plus a fourth—the presence of an absolute zero. This level has a true zero point. In other words, a zero reading means that a zero amount of the trait or characteristic is present. Consider weight, distance, and time for a moment. A box could contain two pounds of candy, one pound of candy, or zero pounds of candy. The concept of zero pounds of candy is meaningful. The same is true of distance and time. Contrast this with zero degrees centigrade or zero degrees Fahrenheit. Do these measurements mean that the system being examined contains no heat at all? Certainly not. A zero point on the scale does not conform to a zero amount of the characteristic being measured. Only in the case of the absolute or Kelvin temperature readings does zero degrees signify zero amount of heat in the system.

As a result of the presence of the absolute zero, ratios between various measurements can be established. For example, clearly a four-pound quantity of candy is twice as much as a two-pound quantity of candy. Also, a person who runs 100 yards in 10 seconds requires one-half as much time as a person who runs 100 yards in 20 seconds. Only in the case of the ratio level of measurement can ratios be established. For example, suppose that we administered a well-developed test of English vocabulary to a group of students. One student had 75 items correct. A second student had 25 items correct. Is it proper to say that the English vocabulary of the first student is three times as large as that of the second student? This statement cannot be made because a student who had zero number of items correct would still, in all probability, have some command of the English language. Since a zero measurement on the scale does not correspond to zero amount of the characteristic being measured, any statement suggesting ratios is inappropriate.

The ratio type of measurement data is not frequently encountered in education. Medical information such as student height and weight is probably the most common instance. Another possibility is the growth or improvement score, that is, the difference between the score of an achievement test administered before an educational experience and that of the same or comparable test administered after the experience. Presumably, a zero growth or improvement score means that the student did not change with regard to those elements of achievement contained in the test. Interpretations such as the foregoing must be tempered by the fact that, since tests do not yield consistent scores, a difference between any two scores from a test is notably inconsistent, that is, unreliable.

Psychological testing. The position of psychological testing with regard to the four levels of measurement can be easily summarized. If well-developed psychological tests which tend to measure a single human characteristic are being applied, the data are generally thought of as falling within the interval level. Of course, if the test is not well-developed, there will be difficulty identifying the level within which the test results fall. Generally, the scores from a poorly designed test are considered to be of the ordinal level of measurement. Some test results, however, are only able to provide nominal level information. In any event, the scores yielded by psychological tests are not of the ratio type. In the interests of efficient testing, the authors of psychological tests design their instruments so that a zero measurement by the test does not conform to zero amount of the trait being measured. Certainly it is not necessary when measuring a student's command of the English language to administer a test which includes every word which he may have learned since birth. Rather, a test is administered which samples his present English vocabulary and which has a floor well above the infant level and a ceiling probably surpassing his present position.

This limitation, the absence of an absolute zero, is not as serious as one might first suppose. Useful as it would be to speak of achievement test results in terms of ratios, the inability to do this is not a grave handicap. More important than the absolute zero characteristic is the equal interval characteristic. In assessing the degree of change in student behavior resulting from educational experiences, the meaning of various differences between scores is the most significant point. For instance, in a longitudinal study of a student's achievement, one would make multiple measurements of that achievement. Hopefully, the score levels would rise each time a test was administered, assuming that formal instruction had occurred between the test administrations. The size of this change is vital information. What does it mean? An answer to this question would require assurance that the measuring instrument used possessed equal intervals.

Citing the level or levels of measurement which are characteristic of the scores yielded by psychological tests is complicated by the fact that the definition of the word "test" is not clearly established. For example, consider the following:[2] A test is defined as *a set of standardized or controlled occasions for response, presented to an individual with design to elicit a representative sample of his behavior when meeting a given kind of environmental demand. The occasion for response most often takes the form of a question or similar verbal stimulus.* In common usage a test is *any set of situations or occasions that elicit a characteristic way of acting, whether or not a task, and whether or not characteristic of the individual's best performance.* The concept "test" is a broad one. Although it is typically used in connection with a paper-and-pencil instrument of the achievement or scholastic aptitude type, the concept includes instruments which are not of the paper-and-pencil type and which do not necessarily reflect degrees of superiority. The variability of tests is illustrated by the descriptions of the types of tests in the following section.

Types of psychological tests. It is surprisingly difficult to classify tests into types. In a number of instances fifteen important types have been identified, and these are not mutually exclusive types. A convenient way of examining the various types is to group them into two's or three's, including in each group types which are more or less contrasting.[3] The fifteen types have been classified into six groups.

---

[2] Horace B. English and Ava C. English, *Comprehensive Dictionary of Psychological and Psychoanalytical Terms* (New York: Longmans, Green & Company, Inc., 1958), p. 547.

[3] J. Stanley Ahmann and Marvin D. Glock, *Evaluating Pupil Growth* (Boston: Allyn & Bacon, Inc., 1959), pp. 63–70.

Informal and standardized tests. Informal tests are teacher-made tests. The teacher makes them for his own classes in order to satisfy his own purposes, as in the case of a spelling, mathematics, or social studies test. These tests are typically achievement tests and are designed to fit a local situation. When properly prepared they can be extremely effective. The reason for this is that a local test has been built for a local purpose.

Standardized tests are typically constructed by a group of individuals and are published and sold commercially. In the case of standardized achievement tests, the subject-matter specialists from all levels of education are a part of a team which also includes test technicians. The content of the test is carefully designed, the questions carefully phrased, and extensive pretesting conducted. These tests are not designed for a particular local situation; rather, they satisfy some or all of the needs of many classroom situations thought to be reasonably similar. A well-known standardized achievement test battery is the Sequential Tests of Educational Progress.

Speed, power, and mastery tests. As the name suggests, a speed test has very rigid time limits. A student is asked to complete a series of exercises, all of which are relatively simple, in a specific length of time. Generally, there are so many of these exercises that he will find it impossible to complete all of them. Those he does complete will probably be correctly completed. The principal characteristics of a speed test are, therefore, a uniformly low level of difficulty of the test items and a short amount of testing time. Clerical aptitude tests in which the student matches names and numbers are examples of speed tests.

Power tests have very comfortable time limits. Rather than containing test items of equivalent difficulty, the power test has a scaled difficulty level. The first test items are relatively easy; the test items which follow become increasingly more difficult; and the test items near the end are so difficult that few students will successfully complete them. Power tests are quite popular in the realm of achievement and aptitude testing, and many standardized achievement tests are essentially power tests. Students, parents, and teachers alike are usually concerned more with the level of attainment of the student when he is given ample time than they are concerned with the speed with which he can accomplish a given task.

A mastery test contains test items with a relatively low level of difficulty, but it still does not restrict, in a highly rigid manner, the time allotted to the student. In a mastery test an attempt is being made only to discover whether or not a student has acquired a given level of competence. There is no desire to determine the degree to which a student surpasses the level of competence represented by the test. Mastery tests are usually informal achievement tests and are used as short quizzes with relatively limited scope, for example, as in the case of the basic skills. Because of the nature of the test, teachers hope that most or all students will answer all test items correctly.

Oral, essay, and objective tests. Oral tests are less popular today than they were a number of years ago. The number of students in a class prevents oral testing from being conducted in the same manner as it was conducted at the turn of the century. Typically, they have been used as achievement tests. Probably their most important use is in connection with evaluating graduate students completing their requirements for a degree. Even in this instance the results they yield are not as consistent as we need.

Essay tests followed naturally from the oral tests. If an instructor found that he did not have time to ask questions individually of each student, he simply wrote the questions on the blackboard and asked the students to write the answers. This is an important change. The essay test does not contain the face-to-face contact which is automatically a part of the oral testing. Hence, the position of the examiner and the examinee are altered. Also, in view of the efficiency of the essay test, the teacher typically prepares the test with far greater care than is true in the case of oral testing. This results in better-quality testing.

Objective tests are probably the most misunderstood type of tests in existence today. Objective tests are not objective in the sense that teacher judgment has been removed from the test construction and the test administration. They are objective only in the sense that they can be *scored* in such a manner that subjective judgment is, for all practical purposes, eliminated. In the case of true-false tests, matching tests, and multiple-choice tests, the answers by the student can be scored objectively. The supply test (for example, the completion test) is called an objective test but does not fully satisfy the requirement of objective scoring. In any event, because of the rapidity with which the tests can be scored, objective tests are the most common type of test used today.

Individual and group tests. A test which must be administered to one student at a time is an individual test. The one-to-one ratio between examiner and student creates a situation which is inefficient in terms of time and cost, but which is extremely efficient in terms of information acquired about the student. A skilled examiner can gain, through an individual test, not only a test score but also a large store of supplementary information, some of which can add immeasurably to the meaning of the total test score. An excellent example of this type of test is the Stanford–Binet Intelligence Scale.

Group tests are administered to more than one student at a time. Because of time and cost considerations, group tests are far more common than individual tests in the public schools today. Achievement testing is completely dominated by the group test. In aptitude testing, a division of use exists between group and individual tests. However, the group test is used more widely.

Verbal, nonverbal, and performance tests. A verbal test is a test in which language is used at some point in its administration. Language could be used in the presentation of the test item, in the directions given to the student, or in the responses made by the student. The use of language simplifies the testing situation. This use occurs whenever possible. In the normal classroom, all achievement and aptitude tests administered are verbal tests.

Nonverbal tests in a strict sense do not require the use of language by either the examiner or the examinee. Communication is established by means of pantomime, and the examinee probably indicates his response with a gesture. These tests have small utility in formal education.

Performance tests are used both in the realm of aptitude testing and in the realm of achievement testing. In both cases the examinee actually performs, that is, he engages in overt motor responses. In the case of aptitude testing, this occurs when a student threads beads on a string, as in the case of the Stanford–Binet Intelligence Scale. In the case of achievement testing, it occurs when the student is engaged in a typing speed test or in a musical performance.

Readiness and diagnostic tests. Readiness tests could be called aptitude tests. Their primary purpose is to predict achievement which would occur if the student were given appropriate training.

Readiness tests are customarily given in the areas of reading and mathematics in the elementary school. Occasionally, they are given at other levels and in other areas.

Diagnostic tests are totally different from readiness tests. The purpose of these tests is to discover the deficiencies in the student's achievement. The teacher is much less interested in total score than he is interested in the response to individual test items or to small groups of test items. Ideally, the diagnostic test contains a cross section of test items that reflect the various aspects of achievement which the student should possess. His inability to answer a test item or a small group of related test items reveals his deficiency and allows diagnosis to be made.

The Nature of Evaluation

The usefulness of psychological tests in education cannot be adequately described without introducing its function in terms of the process of evaluation. When one evaluates, he makes value judgments in terms of standards which he has established. He does this on the basis of available evidence pertinent to the issue under consideration. Tests provide great quantities of this evidence. Although this book is restricted to testing instruments, other types of instruments, such as rating scales and anecdotal records, also contribute in a major way to the evidence used in making a value judgment. Obviously, the evaluator searches for the best possible information which he can find, whether it is produced by tests or by any other instrument. In view of the fact that tests primarily produce quantitative information, they have an advantage over other instruments. However, the fact that the information yielded is quantitative does not necessarily make it more useful to the evaluator. The wise evaluator gathers information from whatever source available, weighs it according to whatever standards he has established, and concludes accordingly.

Evaluation is always oriented toward goals—in this case, educational goals. Formal and informal classroom experiences are organized and presented in terms of appropriate educational objectives. Then the evaluator, that is, the teacher, asks whether the progress of each student is satisfactory. He wishes to know if the student's behavior has changed to an appropriate degree in an appropriate direction. To answer this question, the evaluator must have before him a clear concept of what the educational objectives are.

Educational objectives. Educational objectives stem directly from the needs of youth. Of course, every student needs shelter, food, and rest. He also has needs in the area of his responsibilities as a citizen, his future role as a homemaker and parent, his preparation for earning a livelihood, and his effective utilization of his leisure time. Clearly, he has an extremely large family of needs. Each student, then, has individual versions of these relatively common needs. Some person or organization must assist him in the process of learning how to satisfy his needs. The family in which he is reared, the church and clubs which he attends, and the schools in which he is educated are vital factors in helping him to learn how to satisfy his own needs.

The role of the schools in this process is seldom clearly defined. Moreover, it changes from community to community, because of the varying influence of the family and other organizations which contribute to the process of educating the student. However, a large degree of commonness in the educational objectives exists from school to school. Perhaps the clearest picture of the scope of the educational objectives of today's schools can be obtained by examining an attempt to classify educational objectives.

Taxonomy of educational objectives. Educational objectives can be classified into three domains: the cognitive domain, the affective domain, and the psychomotor domain. The cognitive domain includes those educational objectives which are related to the recall of knowledge and to the development of intellectual abilities and skills. The affective domain includes those objectives which involve changes in student interests, attitudes, values, and appreciations. This is the domain of personal-social adjustment. The psychomotor domain includes objectives related to the motor skill area.

Only the classification of the objectives in the cognitive domain is fully developed. Six major subdivisions of the cognitive domain have been established and these, in turn, are subdivided as needed. An inspection of the subdivisions of the cognitive domain would reveal clearly the hierarchy of the types of educational objectives as they are known to exist. The hierarchy ranges from knowledges, which can involve the simplest type of recall, to evaluation, which includes quantitative and qualitative judgments about the degree to which materials and methods approach criteria which have been established. One can imagine similar systems for the affective and psychomotor domains. The three classifications represent the total framework of educational objectives. They also represent, therefore, the total framework within which evaluation procedures are operating. For every segment of the taxonomy there is, or should be, a segment of evaluation. Hence, a set of evaluation devices, some or all of which are tests, can be constructed. These devices assist in the evaluation process by providing appropriate data on the basis of which the evaluation can be made.

Formal Statements of Educational Objectives

A classification of objectives is not a formulation of objectives. Although only relatively few attempts have been made to classify educational objectives, a large number of individuals and organizations have attempted to formulate educational objectives. Some of the most prominent attempts to do so have resulted in well-received statements of the general objectives of education.[4] Recently, attempts have been made to design statements of the specific objectives of elementary and secondary education. Although not as well known as the general educational objective statements, the statements of specific objectives are more useful in the area of educational evaluation.

Specific objectives of elementary education. Perhaps the most outstanding statement of the specific objectives of elementary education was prepared by the Mid-Century Committee on Outcomes of Education.[5] This committee considered nine curriculum areas: physical development, health, and body care; individual, social, and emotional development; ethical behavior, standards, and values; social relations; the social world; the physical world; esthetic development; communication; quantitative relationships.

[4] "Cardinal Principles of Secondary Education," *United States Office of Education Bulletin* (No. 35, 1918); and Educational Policies Commission, *The Purposes of Education in American Democracy* (Washington, D.C.: National Education Association and the American Association of School Administrators, 1938); and Robert J. Havighurst, *Human Development and Education* (New York: Longmans, Green & Co., Inc., 1953), pp. 25–158.

[5] Nolan C. Kearney, *Elementary School Objectives* (New York: Russell Sage Foundation, 1953), pp. 52–120.

Within each curriculum area four types of student behavioral patterns were cited: knowledges and understandings; skills and competences; attitudes and interests; action patterns.

Finally, objectives were formulated for each behavioral pattern for each curriculum area at three points in time, which are called age-grade periods. These are the primary period, which corresponds to the end of the third grade; the intermediate period, which corresponds to the end of the sixth grade; and the upper-grade period, which corresponds to the end of the ninth grade.

The following are typical of the objectives which are contained in the communication curriculum area. They are appropriate for the intermediate period:

A. Knowledges and understandings.

1. The student has a growing vocabulary of social, scientific, quantitative, physical, esthetic, and technical words: perhaps 7,500 spoken words and 15,000 words comprehended.

2. The student knows the parts of speech, the various kinds of sentences, and the correct letter forms.

B. Skills and competences.

1. The student knows how to look up words, subjects, people, and select and note relevant items.

2. The student participates skillfully in group discussions by listening, speaking, being part of the group, following discussions to their major conclusions, and drawing everyone into the discussion.

C. Attitudes and interests.

1. The student regards reading as an important source of information; he enjoys newspapers and magazines as well as books.

2. The student gets pleasure from composing stories, writing letters, making up rhymes and expressive phrases and sentences.

D. Action patterns.

1. The student voluntarily writes stories and poems and independently proofreads and corrects his own productions, using references when necessary.

2. The student reads in order to be able to contribute to his group or to verify and fortify his opinions and arguments.

Note how the objectives are stated. In each instance they are stated in terms of desired student behavior. This form of statement is essential, primarily because it simplifies the task of the teacher in evaluating the degree to which the objective has been achieved. If he knows clearly what the desired pupil behavior is, and if evalution instruments provide for him a picture of the present state of the student behavior, he is in a position to compare the two and, thus, to make an evaluation.

Specific objectives of secondary education. After the statement of objectives of elementary education had been prepared, a similar study was made of the educational objectives of the secondary school, insofar as general education was concerned. In 1957 the results of this study were published.[6] These objectives are also stated in terms of observable student behavior but are not organized in the same fashion as the elementary school objectives.

The general education objectives of the secondary school are classified under three maturity goals and four areas of behavioral competence.

The maturity goals are: growth toward self-realization; growth toward desirable interpersonal relations in small groups; growth toward effective membership or leadership in large organizations.

The four areas of behavioral competence are: attainment of maximum intellectual growth and development; cultural orientation and integration; physical and mental health; economic competence. Educational objectives have been formulated for each of the four areas of behavioral competence within each of the three maturity goals, thereby making twelve categories of objectives.

Illustrative of the kinds of statements which are included within each of the twelve categories are those statements which are included under the maturity goal of "growth toward self-realization," with respect to the area of behavioral competence known as "attaining maximum intellectual growth and development." The following four objectives are typical of those in this category. All four fall under the general goal of "improving the student's ability to communicate ideas and to recognize and use good standards."

1.121 The student commands and uses the basic skills or reading for information, ideas, opinions, stimulation, and leisure.

1.122 The student expresses his ideas in speech, writing, or in some artistic form with increasing clarity and correctness.

1.123 The student demonstrates his command of quantitative thinking.

1.124 The student is developing some artistic and literary tastes

[6] Will French and Associates, *Behavioral Goals of General Education in High School* (New York: Russell Sage Foundation, 1957), pp. 85–215.

and standards; exhibits creative capacity in some form of worthwhile activities.

For each of these objectives there are listed a large number of behavioral patterns which are illustrative of pupil behavior with regard to this objective. These are most useful in the evaluation process.

Evaluating in Terms of Educational Objectives

The evaluation process is completely tied to educational objectives. The teacher must necessarily teach and evaluate in terms of his educational objectives. If a teacher has relatively few goals and these are of a relatively straightforward nature, his evaluation problems are simplified. On the other hand, if a teacher has a great variety of goals and some, or all, are complex, his evaluation problem becomes more difficult.

The teacher begins the evaluation process by formulating a clear picture of the desired student behavior which will be exhibited if the objective has been achieved. He must also have, of course, a clear concept of other degrees of achievement of the objective, insofar as they are reflected in observable pupil behavior. His task now is to identify the present state of the pupil behavior with regard to the objective under consideration. He needs many tools to assist him in this process. These tools are frequently tests, but they can also be nontest evaluation instruments, for example, rating scales and anecdotal records. It is sometimes difficult to decide which tests or which nontest instruments will yield the best picture of the current state of the pupil's behavior. If possible, several measurements or observations will be made. All too frequently, however, the teacher finds himself in a position whereby he has no evaluation instruments which are totally suitable. Hence, he necessarily improvises and generally reduces the degree of certainty with which he interprets the results of the administration of the evaluation instrument.

Having identified certain goals in terms of which he wishes to evaluate and having identified one or more evaluation instruments to use, the teacher must now provide an opportunity for the student to display his behavior with regard to the goals under consideration. In the case of tests, this is as simple as providing an opportunity for the test to be administered. In the case of nontest instruments, providing the opportunity becomes more difficult in many instances. In any event, the student behavioral patterns must be displayed, and the process of eliciting these behavioral patterns may be such that they are obtained in a natural situation or in an artificial situation.

Student behavior in a natural situation. When student behavioral patterns are elicited in a natural situation, the student is behaving more or less spontaneously to the ordinary course of events. He is behaving as he has learned to behave. He is not experiencing any artificial forces which influence his behavior in an unrealistic manner. This is the ideal fashion in which to observe student behavioral patterns.

As you might guess, it is extremely difficult to arrange situations which provide such a natural setting that the student behavioral patterns elicited are not influenced by artificial forces. Consider for a moment curriculum areas such as communication and ethical behavior. What might be natural situations in which the student will display his communication skills? Does the fact that his handwriting is legible in an assignment submitted to the teacher mean that it will also be legible when he writes a letter from summer camp the following year? Does the fact that his listening skills seem inadequate in the classroom mean that they are equally inadequate when he is in a football huddle? With respect to ethical behavior, we may ask similar questions. What are the natural situations in which a student displays the degree to which he has achieved the objects in the curriculum area of ethical behavior? What are the best opportunities to observe his sportsmanship, his kindliness, or his helpfulness with respect to other people?

While it is true that direct observation of student behavior in a natural situation is the best set of conditions for evaluation, these are not commonly available to the classroom teacher. The limitations of time and opportunity prevent this procedure from having wide utility. Instead, the teacher is compelled to develop artificial situations which resemble natural situations to the greatest possible degree.

Student behavior in an artificial situation. The administration of a test to a student in order to determine his behavioral patterns with respect to a particular educational goal is essentially an artificial situation insofar as evaluation is concerned. This does not necessarily mean that the evaluation is inadequate. It is possible that the degree of similarity between the artificial situation and a corresponding natural situation is so great that the evaluation results yielded by the artificial situation are very similar to those which would have been yielded in a natural situation. The best illustrations of this are found in the so-called academic subjects, that is, those which are verbal or mathematical in nature. Paper-and-pencil tests in reading, vocabulary, and arithmetic computations are of such a nature that they closely approximate the natural situation.

Tests in the cognitive domain with respect to recall of information are probably of similar effectiveness. As we travel through the cognitive domain from the simplest category, knowledge, to the most complex category, evaluation, we find that utility of paper-and-pencil tests has decreased. However, the ingenuity of test builders is such that the loss of utility is far less than many suppose. Both essay tests and some of the more elaborate types of objective tests are able to reveal pupil behavioral patterns in the cognitive domain which are of a complex nature.

Since the cognitive domain is clearly the most important of the three domains, it is not surprising to find that paper-and-pencil testing has dominated the educational scene. To a large degree this is justified. On the other hand, we must remember that nontest devices may, in spite of their technical deficiencies, yield high quality information on the basis of which evaluations can be made. This is true primarily because they can be applied within situations which tend to be less artificial than some of those in which the paper-and-pencil tests are used. Certainly, paper-and-pencil tests should be used only when they will provide the most meaningful information to the student behavioral patterns being evaluated.

The impact of testing on formal education is difficult to comprehend. No one knows the number of informal tests which are constructed and administered each year. With respect to standardized tests, it is estimated that 122 million were administered in the schools of the United States in 1958, as compared with 108 million in 1957 and 100 million in 1956.[7] Included in these figures are tests of achievement, aptitude, and personal-social adjustment. If the results of the test administrations are properly interpreted,

---

[7] Arthur E. Traxler, "Standardized Tests," *National Education Association Journal,* 48 (November 1959), p. 18.

this huge expenditure of student and teacher time is an excellent investment in the national effort to improve the quality and the scope of educational evaluation. Nevertheless, great gains will never be consistently won without the vigorous assistance of nontest evaluation instruments, such as ranking and rating devices, sociometric techniques, questionnaires, and anecdotal records. Although these techniques lack the glittering reputation of tests, they are, nevertheless, indispensable evaluation tools.

CHAPTER II

Constructing Tests

Paper-and-pencil tests are being used with considerable success for measuring degrees of student achievement, aptitude, and personal-social adjustment. The success of the first two areas is particularly pronounced. Informal achievement tests and standardized achievement and aptitude tests are widely administered. Means of constructing these instruments are described in the following sections.

Building Informal Achievement Tests

An excellent view of the many procedures and problems involved in test construction can be obtained by examining the development of an informal achievement test. This development involves an examination and interpretation of educational objectives, the writing of objective or essay test items, and the evaluation of the test after it has been administered.

Role of educational objectives. Paper-and-pencil tests are suitable for providing data on the basis of which a teacher can evaluate the degree to which students have achieved educational objectives of a verbal or mathematical nature. In other words, they are suitable when applied in the cognitive domain. The cognitive domain, as defined by Bloom,[1] is composed of six subdivisions, the first of which is knowledge. Knowledge, in essence, means the ability to recall information upon request. Determining the degree to which students can recall information has been a traditional task assigned to paper-and-pencil tests. The remaining five subdivisions—comprehension, application, analysis, synthesis, and evaluation—may be thought of as parts of a single category known as understanding. The term "understanding," suggests that part of the cognitive domain which is represented by objectives other than those requiring the recall of information per se.

[1] Benjamin S. Bloom, ed., *Taxonomy of Educational Objectives* (New York: Longmans, Green & Co., Inc., 1956), pp. 201–7.

This breakdown of the cognitive domain is helpful in analyzing and interpreting educational objectives. Verbal and mathematical educational objectives commonly identify a quantity of subject matter and relate it to certain desired behavioral changes on the part of the student. These behavioral changes can be thought of in terms of the six subdivisions of the cognitive domain. For purposes of building achievement tests, it is convenient to think of the verbal and mathematical educational objectives in terms of both their subject-matter breakdown and the behavioral change breakdown. This way of thinking automatically forms a two-way grid or table, usually known as the table of specifications. This table provides the outline or blueprint on the basis of which the achievement test is built.

Numerous illustrations of tables of specifications can be found.[2] Typically, they list the breakdown of the subject matter on the vertical axis, whereas the breakdown of the behavioral changes is on the horizontal axis, as shown in Table 1. This table is based primarily on the educational objective. "The student knows the principles of heat transfer and can apply them in new situations."

TABLE 1

TABLE OF SPECIFICATIONS FOR A PHYSICS UNIT DEVOTED TO TRANSFER OF HEAT

	BEHAVIORAL CHANGES		
Subject-Matter Topic	*Recall of Information*	*Application in New Situations*	*Total*
Conduction	25	12	37
Convection	20	6	26
Radiation	25	12	37
Total	70	30	100

In the best judgment of the teacher the subject-matter topics included in this objective, and their relative importance as he sees them, are as follows:

Conduction	37%
Convection	26%
Radiation	37%

[2] Quentin Stodola, *Making the Classroom Test: A Guide for Teachers* (Princeton, N.J.: Educational Testing Service, 1959), pp. 3–14.

For each subject-matter topic he is concerned with two student behavioral changes: the ability to recall information and the ability to apply this information in new situations. In light of the level of the educational experiences presented and the level of student ability and prior achievement, the teacher considers the ability to recall information to be much more important than the ability to apply this information in new situations. It is his opinion that the ratio between the two is 7:3.

Certainly, the foregoing percentages are determined in a highly subjective fashion. They are nothing more than the teacher's opinion of the relative importance of the various categories as they existed in the teaching program. These same degrees of relative importance should exist in the evaluation program. Knowing the manner in which the students have been taught and knowing the abilities of the students, the teacher is in an excellent situation to prepare superior evaluation instruments. For this reason, informal achievement tests, when carefully built, are highly successful devices for providing information on which student achievement can be evaluated.

The subject-matter breakdown, the behavioral change breakdown, and the percentages assigned to their various subcategories are combined to form the table of specifications shown in Table 1. The row and column totals are expressed as percents and are the same as those originally determined by the classroom teacher. The percentages included within the table are rough approximations of the relative importance of each behavioral change in terms of each subject-matter topic. Notice that, of the three subject-matter topics, convection is the least important in the judgment of the teacher. In the case of all three subject-matter topics, the ability to recall information is considered to be much more important than the ability to apply this information to new situations. The least important cell in the entire table is that devoted to the application of information concerning convection in new situations. The implication is that this cell has received least attention in the educational experiences of the students and, therefore, will receive least attention in any evaluation of student achievement.

The test items are constructed in terms of the cells in the table of specifications. For example, in the case of the upper left-hand cell, that is, the cell concerning the ability to recall information with regard to conduction, the following is a suitable test item:

> Which of the following materials is the best conductor of heat?
>
> 1. Silver 3. Silk
> 2. Steel 4. Glass

Since the students had been taught the thermoconductivities of common materials such as the four listed, it is expected that they will identify the first response as the correct response to the multiple-choice test item. Clearly, this is a recall-of-information test item.

Consider for a moment the upper right-hand cell, the cell dealing with the application of conduction information to new situations. A suitable test item for this cell is the following:

> A room measuring 15 × 25 × 8 ft. is insulated on all surfaces by a 4″ covering of glass wool having a thermoconductivity of 7 B.T.U. -in./sq. ft./day/°F. The temperature inside the room is to be maintained at 72°F., while the temperature outside is 50°F. How much heat in terms of B.T.U. must be supplied to this room per hour to offset the loss by conduction?

In view of the fact that the students had not studied the heat loss problem illustrated in the foregoing test item, the test item represents an application of information concerning conduction in a new situation. The ability to repeat information is minimized but still not entirely eliminated. Therefore, it may be the best judgment of the teacher that this item is primarily related to the upper right-hand cell of the table of specifications and secondarily related to the upper left-hand cell of the table. Double relationships such as these between a table of specifications and a test item are relatively common.

It is now evident that the test items are constructed individually and arranged into a test pattern in terms of the table of specifications. In spite of the fact that the percentages included within the table are crude, they do provide a type of guarantee that the test will not be seriously unbalanced. For example, in the case of conduction and radiation, the ratio of approximately 2:1 between ability to recall and ability to apply information is obtained in the test by adding or eliminating test items from the final test form in such a way that the desired balance is present. If the teacher is successful in his efforts to build tests which adequately reflect a well-developed table of specifications, the resulting test will possess a high degree of content validity.

Objective test items. A somewhat perplexing problem which faces the classroom teacher as he prepares to build a test is the selection of the most suitable type of test item to use. He may select essay test items or objective test items. In the latter case, he also must decide which type of objective test item he wishes to use. Objective test items can be thought of as either the supply type of item or as the selection type of item.[3] When responding to the supply type of item, the student must provide the needed words, numbers, or symbols. Possible answers to the test item are not listed. When responding to the selection type of item, the student chooses the correct response from among several possible responses which are provided. Illustrations of this type of item are the true-false test item, the multiple-choice test item, and the matching test item.

On a superficial basis the four principal variations are quite similar. For example, consider the following selection test item.

> The elements fluorine, chlorine, bromine, and iodine are members of the ________ group in the periodic table.

To answer the test item, the student must provide the single word, halogen. Now, let's change the nature of the statement by making it a simple declarative sentence and asking the student to determine whether the statement is true or false. For example:

> The elements fluorine, chlorine, bromine, and iodine are members of the halogen family in the periodic table.

The test item can be changed to a multiple-choice test item by adding distracters or foils, that is, plausible, but wrong, answers to a question or incomplete statement. For example, in the case of the halogen test item, the following is one possibility:

> Which of the following elements is a member of the halogen family?
>
> 1. Helium 3. Potassium
> 2. Iodine 4. Hydrogen

Finally, the multiple-choice test item can be expanded to a matching test item by establishing a list of premises, in this case

---

[3] Robert L. Ebel, "Writing the Test Item," in *Educational Measurement,* ed. E. F. Lindquist (Washington, D.C.: American Council on Education, 1951), p. 193.

families in the periodic table, and a list of responses, in this case a list of elements. The student is to match each premise with one or more of the responses. The following is an example:

Families in the Periodic Table	*Elements*
1. Alkali metals	A. Fluorine
2. Halogens	B. Sodium
3. Inert gases	C. Helium
4. Rare earths	D. Bromine
	E. Rubidium
	F. Iodine
	G. Cerium

In spite of the fact that these changes in format seem relatively minor, the utility of the test item is greatly altered. For example, the multiple-choice test item is capable of reflecting relatively fine discriminations and, therefore, detecting relatively small increments of difference in student achievement. In contrast, the supply test item and the true-false test item typically are not so sensitive in this respect. Moreover, the multiple-choice test item is capable of measuring pupil achievements far more complex than the simple ability to recall information, whereas the supply test item, the true-false test item, and the matching test item are most often used to measure the student's ability to recall information.

Supply test items. The supply test items are questions or incomplete statements which require highly abbreviated answers. One of the most difficult jobs the teacher faces in building this type of test item is to state the test item in such a way that the correct answer is short and specific. There must be only one correct answer, and that answer should be a significant word or expression.

An important advantage of the supply test item is that the possibility of the student's guessing the correct answer is reduced. In the other objective test items the student must only recognize the correct answer. In the case of the supply test item, he must recall it. Paradoxically, this advantage also yields a limitation. No matter how well the teacher may design the supply test item, it seems that the students responding are capable of providing a variety of answers which are only partially correct. For instance, to the test item "San Francisco is a ____," the student may reply "city," "seaport," "place," or "baseball team." Clearly, only the teacher who is intimately familiar with the students and with the educational experiences they have had, can determine the amount of credit to be assigned the student responses. It is in this sense, therefore, that the supply test item is not an objective test item. Strictly speaking, objective test items are those that can be scored in such a way that subjective judgment is eliminated when determining the correctness of a student's response.

A second limitation, which is an outgrowth of the teacher's attempt to design supply test items requiring short and specific answers, is that the test items often involve primarily factual details. Also, there is a heavy emphasis on vocabulary. At some levels of education this type of emphasis is highly desirable. At other levels it is not. In any event, the supply test item commonly demands only recall of information on the part of the student and must be evaluated in this light.

True-false test items. The true-false test item is far more difficult to construct than is commonly supposed. It is not easy to design statements which are true or false without additional qualifications. If the qualifications are added, the statement becomes long and involves a number of important ideas, any one of which may be true or false. This complicates the task of the student's response and may lead to serious confusion. He often wonders whether he should label a test item false if any part of it is false or whether he should label a test item true if it is essentially true in most instances. Thus, how does one respond to the statement, "The White House is the home of all of our presidents"?

In an effort to simplify the test item construction problem, teachers sometimes make the mistake of using "specific determiners" in the statement. These are words or expressions that most often identify the statement contained as either true or false. For example, false statements may contain the expressions "only," "never," "always," or "none." On the other hand, expressions such as "usually," "sometimes," "many," and "frequently" are often found in true statements. If these expressions are used, the observant student will quickly recognize them and select his answer accordingly. Hence, he probably responds correctly to the test item, even though he may not possess the information needed to answer it.

True-false test items are capable of sampling a large amount of subject matter without requiring extreme amounts of testing time. Students can respond to them quickly, provided that the test items are well constructed. Also, the task they face is a practical one. Throughout their lives they will be required to make judgments as to the truth or falsity of statements presented to them. On the other hand, like the supply test item, the true-false test item often is restricted to relatively unimportant information and ideas. Rarely does a true-false test item involve broad generalizations and relationships. When this is attempted, the problem of semantics becomes more and more serious. Hair-splitting distinctions concerning the meaning of the words become important and cause endless debate between teacher and student. Finally, the problem of successful guessing prevents a true-false test item from being considered a highly effective means of determining degrees of student achievement. The student argues that he has an even chance of identifying the correct answer, even though he may not bother to read the statement. Some students are capable of shifting the odds to their favor to a large degree, in spite of very conscientious efforts on the part of the teacher building the test.

Multiple-choice test items. A multiple-choice test item is composed of a stem followed by a series of possible responses or options. The stem is a direct question or an incomplete statement; the options are usually four or five in number, only one of which is the correct response. The incorrect responses are distracters or foils.

The multiple-choice test item has been widely used and widely studied. It is extremely popular in both informal and standardized achievement testing, as well as in standardized aptitude testing. In short, it is a very versatile technique for testing. Its level of difficulty can be varied with relative ease, and it is capable of reflecting simple student behavioral patterns such as recall of information, as well as complex student behavioral patterns such as the ability to analyze and synthesize.

A number of useful variations of the standard type of multiple-choice item have been developed.[4] For example, in some multiple-choice test items, there is more than one correct answer. Or possibly, there is no correct answer. The student must make judgments ac-

---

[4] Paul L. Dressel and J. Schmid, "Some Modifications of the Multiple-Choice Item," *Educational and Psychological Measurement,* 13 (1953), pp. 574–95.

cordingly. Also, attempts have been made to score wrong responses.[5] In this way partial knowledge can be determined at least crudely, and the teacher gains a more intimate view of the command which the student has of the subject matter involved in the test item. Unfortunately, a number of these techniques are difficult to apply in informal achievement testing, but they can be applied in certain standardized tests.

Multiple-choice test items are typically designed so that the stem is relatively long and the options relatively short. One of the most difficult aspects of building multiple-choice test items is to find distracters which are plausible and appealing to those students who do not possess the knowledge or understanding demanded by the test item. These distracters are then stated so that there is grammatical consistency between the options and the stem. The degree to which such consistency strengthens the test item is not as great as once thought.[6]

It has been found that multiple-choice test items can be used at all class levels with the possible exception of the primary class levels. In some instances the actual test is preceded by practice test items administered orally. Other than the area of mathematics, the multiple-choice test item can be used successfully in all subject-matter areas which have verbal and mathematical aspects. Even in the case of mathematics, this type of test item serves a useful function, unless there happens to be a heavy emphasis upon computational aspects of mathematics. If it were not for the fact that the multiple-choice test item is relatively difficult to build, it would probably have replaced most of the other types of objective test items. At the present it is the most important type of objective test item and will likely continue in this role.

Matching test items. The matching test item consists of two,

---

[5] Frederick B. Davis, "Estimation and Use of Scoring Weights for Each Choice of Multiple-Choice Test Items," *Educational and Psychological Measurement,* 19 (Autumn 1959), pp. 291–98; and Frederick B. Davis and G. Fifer, "Effect on Test Reliability and Validity of Scoring Aptitude and Achievement Tests with Weights for Every Choice," *Educational and Psychological Measurement,* 19 (Summer 1959), pp. 159–70; and C. E. Coombs, J. E. Milholland, and F. B. Womer, "The Assessment of Partial Knowledge," *Educational and Psychological Measurement,* 16 (Spring 1956), pp. 13–37.

[6] T. F. Dunn and L. G. Goldstein, "Test Difficulty, Validity, and Reliability as Functions of Selected Multiple-Choice Item Construction Principles," *Educational and Psychological Measurement,* 19 (Summer 1959), pp. 171–79.

occasionally three, lists of items and a set of instructions for matching one of the items in the first list with one or more of the items in the second list. Every effort is made to keep the lists as homogeneous as possible. For instance, one list may be composed of proper names, another of dates, and still another of countries. Thus, a student may match an author with the titles of his published works, statesmen with the countries of their birth, or mathematical symbols with their meaning.

In spite of the fact that lists of homogeneous items are sometimes hard to develop, the matching test item is quite useful for measuring the degree to which the student can recall information. Seldom is the matching test item suitable for measuring the degree to which the student can apply information in a new situation. Generally, students can respond to this type of objective test item quite rapidly, provided that the list of responses is relatively short. For elementary school students, four or five may be the maximum number; for more mature students, the matching test item may be so long that it requires a full page of the test.

Criticisms of objective tests. Criticisms of objective tests have been widespread and have been traced to many sources.[7] In general these criticisms can be reduced to four major categories:

1. Objective tests measure only factual knowledge and fail to measure intellectual skills, such as ability to interpret, ability to analyze critically, and ability to solve problems.
2. Objective test items are often ambiguous, particularly for the better students, and therefore penalize them.
3. Objective tests have a negative effect on teaching, since they encourage the student to learn small bits of knowledge rather than broad understandings and since they discourage writing efforts on the part of the students.
4. Objective tests encourage the student to engage in guessing, a habit which, if deeply engrained, will be hard to change and which may very well yield serious consequences.

There is more than a germ of truth within each of these four criticisms. They are true, to an important degree, in the case of poorly designed and poorly administered objective tests, in both the achievement and aptitude areas. However, their importance can be

---

[7] Henry Chauncey, *Educational Testing Service Annual Report, 1958–1959* (Princeton, N.J.: Educational Testing Service, 1959), pp. 43–57.

greatly reduced if the objective tests are constructed with care and are administered properly.

In the case of the first criticism, it is certainly true that objective tests are an efficient way of measuring the student's ability to recall factual knowledge. There is no significant reason why this should be their only function. Highly successful objective test items have been built which measure more than the student's ability to recall information. For example, a novel situation is posed and one or more objective test items are designed to determine the degree to which the student can interpret and analyze the situation. The novel situation could perhaps be a passage from literature, a law case, a table of meteorological data, a diagram of a malfunctioning television circuit, a map of a fictitious city or country, or a graph or chart showing social and economic trends. The accompanying test items must be constructed so that they can be answered correctly only if the student first recalls the appropriate information and then uses it in terms of the material provided by the description of the novel situation. The student is, therefore, facing a challenging task to which he commonly responds with considerable enthusiasm. This can also be an extremely practical task, provided that the novel situation is a realistic one to him.

The problem of ambiguity, as stated in the second criticism, is certainly one of the most serious facing test builders interested in objective tests. However, it must be remembered that the seriousness of this objection is difficult to assess unless one is intimately familiar with the testing situation and the educational experiences which preceded it. An objective test item taken out of context commonly seems to be very ambiguous in the manner in which it is stated and, therefore, it seems to have either more than one correct answer or no correct answer at all. To the student, however, who perceives the test item in a manner different from that of the layman observer, considerably less ambiguity is present. Nevertheless, the objective test that is completely devoid of ambiguity has never been built. The same can be said for the essay test. The classroom teacher fights an eternal war with this problem of ambiguity. Informal tests which do not have the benefit of pretesting are heavily plagued, in many instances, with ambiguity. On the other hand, standardized tests, if they have been carefully pretested, generally contain such a small amount of ambiguity that the typical student probably finds that he incorrectly interpreted only two per cent or three per cent of the test items administered to him.

The third criticism is in some respects strongly related to the first criticism. As in the case of the first criticism, poorly developed and poorly administered objective tests certainly encourage the students to prepare for them by emphasizing small particles of knowledge rather than broad understandings. This practice will have a serious negative impact on the teaching-learning atmosphere. It is apparent, however, that objective tests which measure both ability to recall information and ability to apply principles will soon correct this improper study procedure on the part of the students.

The doubts about the influence of objective tests on student writing ability are frequently overstated. One learns to write by writing, and it is obvious that students must be provided innumerable opportunities to write. It can be effectively argued that these opportunities to write should not be the relatively brief, infrequent, and emotional periods of time set aside for the administration of tests. Rather, they should be creative efforts which yield work products, for example, themes, compositions, poems, and book reports. These, in turn, provide important data for the evaluation of student achievement.

The problem of student guessing is as persistent a problem as the problem of test item ambiguity. There is no single solution. The conscientious teacher attempts to minimize the magnitude of this problem by administering only carefully developed informal and standardized tests, by penalizing a student for wrong answers, or by both techniques. The question of whether a student should be penalized for wrong answers is difficult to decide. The following is a formula frequently used for this purpose.

$$S = R - \frac{W}{n - 1}$$

where

$S =$ the test score.
$R =$ the number of correct responses.
$W =$ the number of incorrect responses.
$n =$ the number of suggested responses from among which one is chosen.

We must remember that this formula is based upon the assumption that all of the incorrect responses and some of the correct responses are due to the fact that the student guessed wildly. This assumption is, of course, not fully justified. To the degree that it is not justified, the formula is inappropriate.

Finally, it must be remembered that if every student answers every test item, we may as well not correct for guessing. In this case test scores determined by counting the number of correct responses are correlated perfectly with those computed by applying the correction-for-guessing formula. Bear in mind that the foregoing statement does not mean that, for each student, the two scores computed are identical. Instead, it means that the relative position of each student in the class is the same in terms of the two distributions of test scores. It is for this reason that some teachers argue that the simpler test score (that is, the number of correct responses) may as well be used. Research concerning this and other aspects of the usefulness of correcting for guessing is continuing.[8]

Essay test items. In the case of the essay test item the student does not elect the test answer but must supply it, and that answer is usually one or more sentences. The accuracy and quality of each answer must be judged subjectively by a person skilled and informed of the subject matter, customarily the classroom teacher.[9]

For many years the essay test item has been the mainstay of paper-and-pencil testing. Its role today is often misunderstood. Rather than being totally replaced by the objective test item, as some suppose, it has simply released part of its function to the objective test item and is performing the remainder of its functions as effectively as before. That part which has been released is the part devoted to the measurement of the student's ability to recall information. It is in this area that the objective test item is extremely efficient. The informed teacher today is using objective test items primarily for this purpose and is using essay test items primarily for the purpose of measuring higher-level intellectual skills of the

---

[8] Frederick B. Davis, "Use of Correction for Chance Success in Test Scoring," *Journal of Educational Research,* 52 (March 1959), pp. 279–80; and R. A. Jackson, "Guessing and Test Performance," *Educational and Psychological Measurement,* 15 (Spring 1955), pp. 74–79.

[9] John M. Stalnaker, "The Essay Type of Examination," in *Educational Measurement,* ed. E. F. Lindquist (Washington, D.C.: American Council on Education, 1951), pp. 495–530.

student. The essay test item is well suited for this type of function, provided that it is designed so that the student response is reasonably restricted. Student responses of unrestricted length are usually so difficult to score that the effectiveness of the essay test item as an evaluation technique becomes virtually nil.

Constructing essay test items. On the surface, the essay test item seems very simple to construct. While it is true that the technique of constructing essay test items is more easily acquired than the technique of constructing the objective test items, essay test items are more complex than they seem. For example, a science teacher might say to his students, "Describe what happens when there is an eclipse of the moon." To this, one student responds, "Lots of people go outside to look at it." In a similar situation was the social studies teacher who inquired, "What caused the downfall of the Roman Empire?" One student response was a single word: "Carelessness." How are these responses to be scored? In a sense, they are not incorrect answers, yet they certainly are not the answers intended.

To prevent difficulties in scoring, it is necessary to design essay test items in as careful a manner as possible. Both of the foregoing questions could be greatly improved. In each case the essay test item should be lengthened in such a way that it specifies more clearly its intent. The first test item should be worded so that it is abundantly clear that the teacher wants to know what happens to the moon, earth, and sun at the time of an eclipse rather, than what happens to the people who are aware of the occurrence. An improved statement of this essay test item is the following: "Explain the eclipse of the moon in terms of the position and direction of movement of the moon, earth, and sun."

The foregoing examples illustrate a common problem of constructing essay test items, namely, a reluctance to stipulate clearly and concisely the intent of the test item. Making this stipulation allows the student to grasp immediately and without difficulty the test item's intent. Any difficulty which the student experiences as he writes an essay test should not be traceable to understanding the intent of the given item, but to formulating an answer to that item once he understands its intent. To help the student understand, the statement of the essay test item is commonly relatively long, perhaps two or three sentences. If this length is properly used, the student will be able to see the essay test item as an organized whole, thereby being able to plan his answer systematically and to restrict his response to pertinent matters only.

Scoring the essay test item. The most difficult aspect of essay testing is not the construction of the test item, but the scoring of the student response. The two are, of course, highly related. An essay test item worded so that the student's response can vary considerably and still be, in a sense, correct means that the scoring problem is unmanageable. On the other hand, essay test items constructed so that the student's response is relatively restricted will produce a scoring situation which is reasonable. In any event, it is a disagreeable task.

For more reliable scoring, teachers make every effort to score the responses of the students anonymously and to score all the responses of a given test item at one time. Should they be in doubt about their impartiality, they may even consult a second party, who then scores the student responses independently. In addition, penmanship, grammar, spelling, and style of writing should be scored separate from the subject-matter content of the responses. This in no way suggests that the writing aspects of the responses are not important. It simply means that these are different from the subject-matter content, and in order to analyze with clarity the student's achievement, they must be scored independently.

A popular manner of scoring responses of essay test items is the rating technique. The teacher attempts to grasp the wholeness of the student's response and to rate it as good, average, or poor. This technique is repeated for each test item and the results of all test items are summarized as a total score.

A more reliable and more complex system is the analytical method. The correct response to the test item is broken down into its component parts, and the total number of raw-score points allowed for the correct response is distributed among the various component parts, according to the teacher's best judgment of the matter. Each pupil's response is then analyzed in terms of each subpart. For every subpart properly handled the student receives the appropriate number of raw-score points. Extraneous material is ignored. For instance, in the case of the lunar eclipse test item, the student must explicitly say that the moon is in the earth's shadow in order to gain whatever credit is allowed.

The analytical scoring system works quite well. Those who use it quickly find that it is most satisfactory for essay test items which are designed to elicit relatively restricted student responses. In an attempt to relieve the scoring burden, teachers frequently redesign the statement of their essay test items. In most instances, this is a much needed improvement.

Comparison of objective and essay tests. Neither the objective test item nor the essay test item is unquestionably superior or inferior to the other. Although each type of test item can perform all of the functions of the other, it cannot perform those functions with the same efficiency. It is not surprising, therefore, that teachers frequently use informal achievement tests which involve both objective and essay test items, with the essay test items placed last in the test. This allows considerable flexibility in test item construction and provides a challenging, meaningful task for the student.

It is helpful to compare objective and essay tests in terms of their general characteristics. A summary of this comparison is shown in Table 2.[10] Inspection of this table quickly reveals that each type of test has unique advantages and limitations. By judiciously using both types of test items the teacher can capitalize on the advantages of each and minimize the influence of their limitations.

Item Analysis of Test Results

Student responses to objective test items are studied in order to determine the relative difficulty and discriminating power of the test item. This process is known as item analysis. It can also be applied to essay test item responses, provided that they are scored by the analytical method; but this is a difficult process. In either case, the primary purpose of the item analysis is to improve the quality of the test item for future administration. A second purpose of considerable importance is to study the strengths and weaknesses in the academic achievement of the students who have responded to the test item. By studying the nature of the incorrect responses, the teacher is able to gain a superior view of the relative position of each student with regard to the material being tested.

---

[10] J. Stanley Ahmann and Marvin D. Glock, *Evaluating Pupil Growth* (Boston: Allyn & Bacon, Inc., 1959), p. 286.

TABLE 2

COMPARISON OF ESSAY AND OBJECTIVE TESTS

Characteristic	*Essay Test*	*Objective Test*
Preparation of the test item.	Items are relatively easy to construct.	Items are relatively difficult to construct.
Sampling of the subject matter.	Sampling is often limited.	Sampling is usually extensive.
Measurement of knowledges and understandings.	Items can measure both; measurement of understanding is recommended.	Items can measure both; measurement of knowledges is emphasized.
Preparation by pupil.	Emphasis is primarily on larger units of material.	Emphasis is primarily on factual details.
Nature of response by pupil.	Pupil organizes original response.	Except for supply test items, pupil selects response.
Guessing of correct response by pupil.	Successful guessing is minor problem.	Successful guessing is major problem.
Scoring of pupil responses.	Scoring is difficult, time-consuming, and somewhat unreliable.	Scoring is simple, rapid, and highly reliable.

Test item difficulty. By test item difficulty is meant the per cent of students who correctly answer to a given test item. This information is of little value to the teacher when a mastery test is under consideration, but it can be of great help to him if he is concerned with a power test, that is, a test which is to yield scores on the basis of which students are to be ranked in terms of their achievement.

Determining the level of difficulty of a test item is a relatively easy task. The following formula is used:

$$P = \frac{N_r}{N_t} (100)$$

where

P = percentage of students who answered the test item correctly.

N_r = number of students who answer the test item correctly.

N_t = total number of students who attempt to answer the test item.

For each test item the appropriate entries are made into the formula and the formula is solved. The resulting percentages can, of course, range from 0 to 100. It is most desirable that the percentages cluster around the 50 per cent level. Generally they are lower than 30 per cent and greater than 70 per cent only in rare instances in the case of well-developed tests. Test items which are extremely difficult or extremely easy do not help, to any noticeable degree, in the process of attempting to differentiate among students in terms of their achievement. The only important use of test items with levels of difficulty near 100 per cent is to place them at the beginning of a test in order to introduce the student to the remainder of the test in a somewhat gentle fashion.

Sometimes it is convenient to compute the difficulties of test items without having the information needed for all of the students to whom the test is administered. Instead, the item difficulties are computed on the basis of the responses made by those students who have achieved very well and those students who have achieved rather poorly.[11] The middle group is discarded. The approximations of the *P*-values which result are in many cases quite suitable for interpretation purposes.

Test item discriminating power. A test item possesses adequate discriminating power when it is capable of differentiating between superior and inferior students. The superior group (commonly known as the upper group) and the inferior group (commonly known as the lower group) can be identified in any number of different ways. Independent criteria such as standardized test results, final marks, or teacher ratings and rankings have seldom been used because of their unavailability. More commonly, an internal criterion is used. This criterion is the total score which the student received on the test which contains the test item whose discriminating power is to be determined. In other words, the test scores from the test containing the test item of interest are arranged from high to low. A small segment of the higher scores and a small segment of the lower scores are used to identify the upper group and the lower group. All other students are ignored, insofar as the process of determining item discriminating power is concerned. The size of the upper group and the lower group can vary, but it generally does not. Usually each is 27 per cent of the total group.

Many different computational schemes have been proposed which will provide indexes of discriminating power for a given test item.

[11] E. L. Clark, "Item Difficulties Based on End Segments," *Journal of Educational Psychology,* 48 (November 1957), pp. 457–59.

Some of these are quite complex and, therefore, are used only in the case of standardized test construction procedures. Others involve only a few simple arithmetic steps. An illustration of this is the following:[12]

$$D = \frac{U - L}{N}$$

where

D = index of item discriminating power.
U = number of students in the upper group who answer the test item correctly.
L = number of students in the lower group who answer the test item correctly.
N = number of students in each group.

The maximum size of the *D*-values is + 1.00 and the minimum size is — 1.00. The former indicates maximum discriminating power in the desired direction, whereas the latter indicates that discrimination occurs in the opposite direction of that desired. Any negative *D*-value indicates that the test item is discriminating to some degree in the wrong direction. Obviously, therefore, the interest is in test items which yield *D*-values which are positive. Those *D*-values which exceed + 0.40 are good; those between + 0.40 and + 0.20 are satisfactory; and those between + 0.20 and 0 are poor.

Ebel[13] suggests that in the case of a well-developed achievement test, more than 50 per cent of the test items should have *D*-values exceeding + 0.40; less than 40 per cent should have *D*-values between + 0.40 and + 0.20; and less than 10 per cent should have values between + 0.20 and 0. There should be no negative *D*-values.

In his study of the utility of a test item, the skilled test builder tries to go beyond such summary values as a *P*-value and a *D*-value. He examines with care the responses made to each test item. For example, in the case of a multiple-choice test item he scrutinizes not only the degree to which students responded correctly but also

[12] A. Pemberton Johnson, "Notes on a Suggested Index of Item Validity: The U-L Index," *Journal of Educational Psychology,* 42 (December 1951), pp. 499–504; and Warren G. Findley, "A Rationale for Evaluation of Item Discrimination Statistics," *Educational and Psychological Measurement,* 16 (Summer 1956), pp. 175–80.

[13] Robert L. Ebel, "Procedures for the Analysis of Classroom Tests," *Educational and Psychological Measurement,* 14 (Summer 1954), pp. 352–64.

the responses to all of the distracters. Subtle weaknesses in the test item may appear. It is possible that a test item with a satisfactory *P*-value and *D*-value will still have distracters, which are, for all practical purposes, nonfunctional. Students may seldom choose them, or the distracter will not have a differential attractiveness, that is, a greater attractiveness to the lower group than to the upper group. Editing or eliminating such distracters will strengthen the test item and, therefore, the test in which it appears.

Building Standardized Tests

There is considerable similarity between the procedure used to construct standardized achievement tests and that used to construct standardized aptitude tests. Hence, it is appropriate to consider these procedures simultaneously. They can be summarized within three main categories: planning and writing the test, pretesting and analyzing the results, and norming the test.

Planning and writing the test. Standardized tests are the outgrowth of the intense and widespread testing need on the part of educational institutions with respect to a particular problem or set of problems they are facing, for example, as in the case of determining changes in a student's command of his basic skills as he progresses through elementary school. Only when the need is of this nature is there sufficient justification for the expense and effort of constructing a standardized test. As the need crystallizes, it, in effect, forms the program or outline for the test.

Representatives of the various educational groups who express the need mentioned are organized for the purpose of identifying specifically what goals the test should accomplish. These representatives set up the specifications for the test, that is, the abilities, the skills, or the types of information which the test should attempt to measure. They also indicate the purposes which the test results will serve and the kinds of students to which the test should be administered.

In the case of achievement tests, the specifications set up by the representatives are outlined in considerable detail. The types of subject matter to be covered and the types of behavioral changes of the students to be sampled are carefully cross referenced by means of tables of specifications. The educational representatives, with the help of other subject-matter specialists and testing technicians, then formulate test items which are reviewed and edited.

The test item writing procedure is somewhat different in the case of aptitude tests, such as a mental ability test. Here, the test technicians write the items. However, before they can be certain as to exactly which student characteristics they are measuring, it is sometimes necessary for considerable research to precede the test item writing stage as well as to follow that stage, and, hence, to contribute to later test item writing attempts. It is at this point that factor analysis becomes a highly useful tool to test builders. The factor analysis could be any one of a number of complex mathematical methods of analyzing tests or the relationships among tests for the purpose of obtaining ideas about the psychological traits or factors displayed by the students tested. Relationships among several tests can be described in terms of the smallest possible number of traits or factors. For a single test the test builder can discover the nature of the underlying psychological processes which determine the results yielded by that test.[14]

Pretesting and analyzing the results. The first "tryout" form of the test is called a pretest. Usually, it is longer than the final test is to be. Although all of the items within the pretest are thought to have considerable potential, it is recognized that a fairly large per cent of them will prove to be unsatisfactory for one reason or another. Hence, the pretest is administered to a group of students who are typical of those for whom the test is being built. It is most important that this group represent all of the variations in ability and all of the variations with respect to cultural advantages and disadvantages which are thought to be present in the target population. Also, the testing conditions are carefully controlled so that they too may be considered typical of those which will exist when the final form of the test is administered.

The student responses to the various test items are studied with great care. Important information is that concerning the level of difficulty of each item and the discriminating power of each item. The former is determined by discovering the per cent of students who correctly answered the item. The latter is determined by dis-

---

[14] Carter V. Good, ed., *Dictionary of Education,* 2nd ed. (New York: McGraw-Hill Book Co., Inc., 1959), p. 221.

covering which items discriminate between the superior students and the inferior students.

Test items which are rarely answered correctly or which are almost always answered correctly are edited so as to change the level of difficulty so that it conforms more closely to 50 per cent. It is hoped that the final form of the test will be of such a nature that the average student in a class for which the test is designed will answer slightly more than one-half of the test items correctly. Insofar as item discrimination power is concerned, useful test items should have a "positive" discriminating power. By this is meant that superior students will tend to answer it correctly in greater numbers than will inferior students. Those test items with negative discriminating power are either discarded or edited to change their discriminating power to conform to the positive direction.

On the basis of the results yielded by the foregoing analyses (that is, item analyses), a final form of the test is assembled. To be certain that this form adheres to the specifications originally established by the educational representatives, the test is again critically reviewed by test technicians, educational personnel, and other qualified outside consultants.

Norming the test. At such time as the final form of the test is judged to be satisfactory, it is administered to a sample of students typical of those for whom the test is originally designed. The scores of these students are classified into reasonably homogeneous groups according to pertinent student characteristics such as age, class level, type of school, type of curriculum, and geographical area. The test results are arranged in tables in such a way as to provide a basis upon which comparisons can be made between a test score by a given student and the typical performance made by this sample of students. These tables are called tables of norms and can take many different forms, such as percentile rank and grade equivalents. Basically their purpose is to allow a student or teacher to identify the relative performance of any given student or class of students.

In addition to the original form of the test, a second or equivalent form of the test is often developed. The second form is of such a nature that its scores can be interpreted in the same way as the scores on the original form. The presence of two forms allows greater administrative flexibility in the use of tests in the typical school situation. Ideally, the tables of norms for both forms are identical.

Needless to say, the construction of a standardized test never really ends. As additional information concerning its suitability and accuracy becomes available, revisions of the original test become necessary. To be of most use standardized tests must be up to date. This is particularly true of achievement tests and, consequently, editions follow editions with considerable regularity in this testing area.

CHAPTER III

Test Reliability, Validity, and Norms

The history of man's efforts to measure the physical phenomena which surround him is indeed a fascinating one. In the case of measurement of distance, as recently as the sixteenth century men were defining distances in heel-to-toe methods. For instance, in Germany in that era a measure of length known as the rute was defined as that distance determined by sixteen men lined up heel-to-toe. This measurement was the same as the English rod and was a satisfactory measurement for that time. However, by 1875 it was necessary to be more specific. In that year 28 nations adopted the standard meter bar. This is a platinum-iridium alloy bar with two microscopically thin lines near each end, the distance between them being exactly one meter.

Although this bar allows measurements with an accuracy of 1 part in 10 million, it is not a suitable standard for the space age. Consequently, in 1960 a new official standard of length was adopted, determined in terms of a wave length of light. Now the meter is defined as 1,650,763.73 wave lengths of the orange-red light given off by electrically excited krypton 86. This new standard permits measurements of distance to be made which are accurate to 1 part in 100 million. Since it is customarily expected that a master standard must be at least ten times more accurate than the practical measuring devices based upon it, it is necessary that this extremely high degree of accuracy be maintained in order to permit important technological advances.

Facts such as these concerning the degree of accuracy which presently exists in the physical and biological sciences impresses upon us the relative lack of accuracy which exists in measuring attempts in the behavioral sciences. The measurement process in the behavioral sciences, beginning in the first part of the twentieth century, has made giant strides but still is plagued with innumerable errors, some of which can be of considerable magnitude. To appreciate the role which this measurement can play in professional education, we must be well-informed about the nature of the errors which commonly occur in psychological measurement.

Errors in Psychological Testing

The errors which exist in psychological testing can be classified into two major categories and these, in turn, can be divided into various subcategories. The two major categories of errors are *compensating errors* and *biased errors.* Compensating errors are sometimes known as chance or accidental errors. They possess one important characteristic: If many measurement attempts are made, these errors will tend to cancel each other. Biased errors do not possess this characteristic. No matter how many measurement attempts are made, no tendency for the errors to cancel each other is discernible.

Compensating errors. There are three types of compensating errors:[1]

1. Failure to include an infinite number of test items in the test.
2. Failure to administer the test to the students an infinite number of times.
3. Failure to utilize an infinite number of judges when scoring the student responses.

The first of these three compensating errors refers to the test itself. The second refers to the students to whom the test is administered, and the third refers to the scorers of the student responses.

In the case of the first error, a test is necessarily a sample of a large population of test items which might have been used. Whenever a population is sampled, the influence of chance on the nature of the sample must be considered. Two samples randomly drawn from the same population (that is, drawn so that every member of the population has an equal opportunity of being a member of the sample) will, in all probability, differ at least slightly because of chance. If countless random samples were to be drawn and their characteristics examined, their tendency to overestimate and to un-

[1] James E. Wert, Charles O. Neidt, and J. Stanley Ahmann, *Statistical Methods in Educational and Psychological Research* (New York: Appleton-Century-Crofts, Inc., 1954), p. 325.

derestimate a certain characteristic of the population would be essentially equal. This same phenomenon exists in the case of tests. Since there is but one test and it does not include all items within the population of test items, chance error is present.

Whereas the first compensating error is a test-centered error, the second is a student-centered error. In many subtle ways students differ from one test administration to another. It is possible that their state of health, their motivation, or their emotional stability varies to important degrees from even morning to afternoon. These variations could produce important differences in test results, although in the majority of instances they probably do not. Depending upon the state of the student at the time of test administration, his success may be enhanced or reduced. If it were possible to test him an infinite number of times, these variations would probably cancel each other, leaving a clear picture of typical performance on the part of the student.

The third compensating error is the scorer error. In the case of objective test items it probably is so small that it is not worthy of mention. In the case of essay test items the element of chance in the scoring of the student responses is probably larger and, therefore, the degree of error is probably larger. To prevent this error, scorers must be able to reproduce their evaluations of the student's performance without variations. If it were possible to employ an infinite number of judges to score all of the responses, it is argued that any tendency to allow too much credit or too little credit to a given student's response would be canceled.

Biased errors. Five important biased errors can be listed:[2]

1. Failure to break down the student attribute to be measured to the point where it is homogeneous.
2. Failure to choose test items that measure the characteristic in question.
3. Failure to choose a good cross section of test items.
4. Failure to weight the test items in accordance with their importance.
5. Failure to score the test honestly.

The first four of these errors can be traced to the test construction process, whereas the fifth is a question of scorer honesty. Some of the most satisfactory psychological tests attempt to measure a single

[2] *Ibid.*, pp. 325–27.

homogeneous student characteristic insofar as it is possible to identify such a characteristic. A test that attempts to measure a number of student characteristics, even though those characteristics may be related to each other to a noticeable degree, is typically one which produces total scores of limited interpretability. Rarely is the relative importance of the traits known insofar as the contribution of the traits to the total score is concerned. Factor-analytic studies of tests assist in the interpretation of test scores by identifying those relatively unrelated factors or traits which contribute to the scores. Although the first biased error is difficult to avoid because human performance reflects a combination of human traits, the error can be reduced by carefully building subtests aimed at specific student characteristics.

The second biased error is an obvious one, yet test builders sometimes feel a bit helpless concerning it. For instance, they may wonder whether the test item which has been designed to measure the student's ability to apply information in a new situation actually does measure that student ability. It is possible that, for a given student, the item is nothing more than a recall of information item because the situation does not happen to be a novel one insofar as he is concerned. Since the test builder is incapable of controlling possibilities such as this, he recognizes that the second type of error is present to some degree in his instrument.

The question of a good cross section of test items, as mentioned in the third type of biased error, renews the question of sampling a population of possible test items. Random samples are subject to compensating error but not to biased error. On the other hand, samples haphazardly drawn, as is so often true of informal achievement tests, contain both biased and compensating errors. Since the theoretical population of test items concerning a particular student characteristic cannot be sampled so that every test item has an equal opportunity of being a part of the test (that is, the sample), we know that our tests are not random samples. Are such samples of test items cross-sectional samples? In the case of achievement testing, the table of specifications is used so that this question can be answered affirmatively. If the table is carefully designed in terms of appropriate educational objectives, and if the test items are carefully constructed and cross referenced with this table, then the teacher has reasonable assurance that his test is a cross section of the subject matter and the student behavioral changes which are important to him.

The fourth biased error is also a common one. Experience in testing reveals most clearly that each test item is not of the same importance as all other test items contained in a given test. No doubt the exact contribution of each test item to the process of measuring the student characteristic in question does vary noticeably from item to item. Generally speaking, however, the exact contribution of each test item is unknown, and the problem of weighting the test items in accordance to their importance is solved by simply assigning equal weights to all items. Theoretically, this cannot be justified. Actually, the errors inherent in this process seem to be much less important than one would expect.

The final biased error—the failure to score the student responses honestly—is a question of proper training for test scorers. Here again, the problem with respect to the objective test is not an important one. Difficulties in scoring responses to the essay test item are well-known and represent an excellent illustration of this biased error. Test scorers of essay responses who allow themselves to be influenced by legible handwriting, smooth flowing prose, and a favorable interpersonal relationship with the student will misrepresent the quality of the student's response if it is to be evaluated on the basis of his command of the subject matter. Remember that, for a given scorer, this error is not a compensating one. Irrespective of whether or not this misrepresentation is more unconscious than conscious, or in a negative direction rather than in a positive direction, the error exists in a given direction and is potentially serious.

Definition of reliability and validity. The degree to which a given test is probably influenced by compensating and biased errors is reflected in the degree to which that test is reliable and valid. Although test specialists do not completely agree on the relationship between the various types of errors and the concepts of reliability and validity, it is very helpful to think of the errors in terms of these two concepts. Test reliability is commonly thought of as the degree to which the test is free of compensating errors.[3] On the other hand,

---

[3] Robert L. Thorndike, "Reliability," in *Educational Measurement,* ed. E. F. Lindquist (Washington, D.C.: American Council on Education, 1951), pp. 560–620.

test validity is often considered to be the degree to which the test is free of both compensating and biased errors. If one accepts these definitions, he automatically accepts the fact that although the role of test reliability is a vital one, it is still distinctly secondary to the role of test validity when a psychological test is being appraised. Moreover, if a test is highly valid, it must possess a considerable degree of reliability; indeed, the unreliability of a test in reality forms an upper limit for the maximum validity which the test can possess.

A highly reliable psychological test yields consistent test results. If it is administered repeatedly in an unchanging situation, the test results are constant or nearly constant. Scorer reliability is a part of the over-all test reliability. It is the degree to which the third compensating error is absent. Since it deals with the assigning of credit to student responses, and not with the construction of the test itself, some evaluation specialists study it separately, especially in the areas of nontest instruments.

Test validity is typically defined as the degree to which the test actually serves the purposes for which it is intended. In effect, this definition says that there are many different kinds of test validity. As the purposes of the test change, so does the degree to which it is valid. A test may be highly valid for one purpose, moderately valid for other purposes, and totally invalid for still other purposes. A clear picture of this must be presented to the test user before proper administration and interpretation can take place.

Determining Degrees of Reliability

The traditional manner of determining the reliability of a test is to administer that test at least twice to a group of students, with the expectation that the students have not changed during the time interval between the two administrations with regard to the characteristic being measured. If the test is perfectly reliable, the two scores for any student will be identical. In reality this does not happen very often. Instead, highly reliable tests will yield results which place the student in the same relative position with regard to his classmates at one administration as it will at any other administration, provided, of course, that the students have not changed with regard to the characteristic being measured.

The degree to which a test is reliable can be represented by a coefficient of reliability. There are four types of such coefficients: coefficients of stability; coefficients of equivalence; coefficients of stability and equivalence; and coefficients of internal consistency.[4] When several reliability determinations have been made, one may find that several different types of coefficients have been computed.

Coefficient of stability. Imagine that a test which is highly reliable is administered twice to the same group of students and that a scatter diagram of the test scores is plotted. Such a diagram would resemble that shown in Figure 1. If you examine the diagram carefully you will notice that only a minority of students evidently received the same test score for the two test administrations. However, variations in the sizes of the test scores are small. As a result, the scatter diagram reveals an elongated pattern which strongly resembles a straight line. As the tendency to resemble a straight line increases, the reliability of the test increases; as the tendency to resemble a straight line decreases, the reliability of the test decreases.

A convenient means of representing succinctly the degree to which a series of dots (such as shown in Figure 1) resemble a straight line is the product-moment coefficient of correlation. This coefficient is represented by the letter "r" and varies in size from a positive 1.00 to a negative 1.00. If all of the dots in Figure 1 conformed perfectly to a straight line, the coefficient of correlation would be + 1.00. On the other hand, if they were scattered evenly throughout the figure in such a way that one could detect virtually no tendency to conform to a single straight line, then the coefficient would be in the vicinity of 0.00. The coefficient for Figure 1 is about + 0.87, which is typical of standardized achievement tests.

The results of administering a given test twice to the same group of students with a relatively short time interval between the two test administrations can be represented by a coefficient of correlation known as a coefficient of stability. Although there are certain limitations to this type of reliability determination, it still remains an extremely popular method of determining test reliability.

---

[4] American Psychological Association, American Educational Research Association, and National Council on Measurements Used in Education, "Technical Recommendations for Psychological Tests and Diagnostic Techniques," Supplement to the *Psychological Bulletin,* 51, Part 2 (March 1954), pp. 28–33.

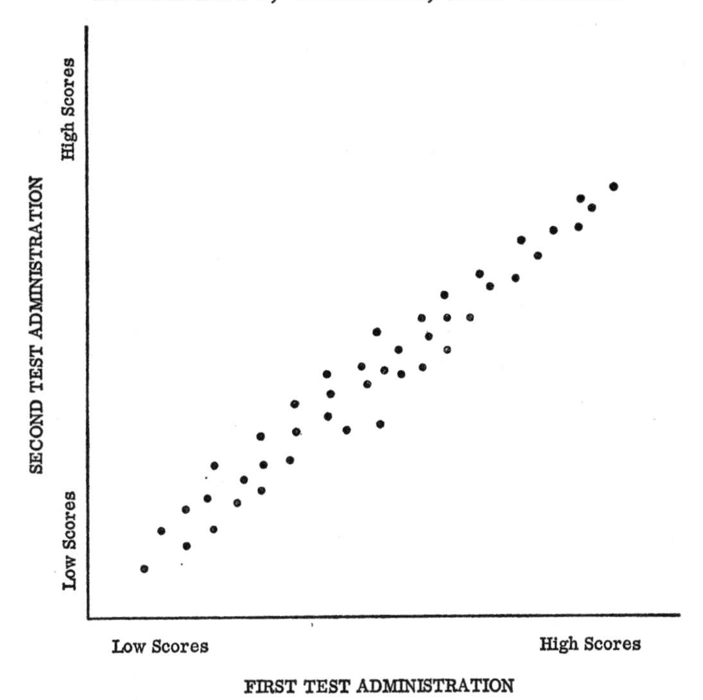

Figure 1. Scatter Diagram of Test Scores Resulting from Two Test Administrations.

Coefficient of equivalence. Another means of determining the degree to which a test is reliable is the computation of a coefficient of equivalence. This also is a coefficient of correlation but is based upon the test results yielded by two equivalent forms of a test rather than upon a double administration of one test. Equivalent forms are often difficult to build and for this reason are available only in the case of a standardized test. Equivalent tests are two independent samples of the same population of test items. They are supposed to measure the same student characteristics but have a completely different set of test items. Hence, the test scores yielded by two equivalent forms of a test should be of the same size for a given student and should be interpreted in the same manner.

Suppose that a group of students were administered two equivalent forms of a test with only a very brief rest period between the two test administrations. In the case of well-constructed tests the scatter diagram of the results would resemble that shown in Figure 1. Students who performed poorly on the first form would also perform poorly on the second form; those who performed well on the first form would also perform well on the second form. A coefficient of correlation computed on the basis of these data is a coefficient of reliability known as a coefficient of equivalence. However, it is different from the coefficient of stability in that it reflects the degree to which the first compensating error (the test-centered error) is absent, whereas the coefficient of stability reflects the degree to which the second compensating error (the student-centered error) is absent.

Coefficient of stability and equivalence. It is possible, of course, to combine the two foregoing techniques when determining the degree of reliability of a test. One can use two equivalent forms and administer them with a sizeable time interval between the two test administrations. The results could be plotted as a scatter diagram.

The coefficient of correlation which is computed when the data are produced by two equivalent forms administered with a noticeable time interval between the two test administrations is known as a coefficient of stability and equivalence. It is a superior means of determining the degree of test reliability which exists, since it reflects both the test-centered and student-centered errors. In view of the fact that the two equivalent forms represent two independent samples of a population of possible test items, and the two test administrations represent a sample of a population of many possible test administrations, both types of compensating error are allowed to manifest themselves in the test results.

Coefficient of internal consistency. The foregoing three methods of determining the degree of test reliability require important investments of time and effort in order to achieve interpretable results. In an effort to simplify the determination of the degree of test reliability which exist, short-cut techniques have been developed and are frequently used. These are based on a single form of the test which is to be administered only once. The analysis of the data is also based upon the computation of a coefficient of correlation, this coefficient being known as a coefficient of internal consistency.

Two formulas are commonly used in the computation of a coefficient of internal consistency. These differ from the traditional method of computing a coefficient of correlation. One of them is known as the Spearman-Brown "Prophecy Formula."[5] Basic information for this formula is the coefficient of correlation between the scores yielded by the odd-numbered items and the scores yielded by the even-numbered items. In other words, the test is imagined to be two subtests, each one-half the size of the original test.

Also available to the test builder who wishes to determine a coefficient of internal consistency are the Kuder-Richardson formulas.[6] The computation of this coefficient of internal consistency is not based upon any artificial division of the test, but rather upon the proportion of students failing and the proportion of students passing each test item. Like the coefficients of correlation yielded by the Spearman-Brown formula, the Kuder-Richardson coefficients are not meaningful when based upon a speed test, but are meaningful when based upon a power test. In the case of speed tests the coefficients are unrealistically large.

Standard error of measurement. It is convenient to represent the degree to which a test is reliable by identifying the size of the error which probably exists in a given test score because of the unreliability of the test. This error is known as the standard error of measurement.[7] The computation of the standard error of measurement requires that a coefficient of reliability be known. The larger the coefficient of reliability, the smaller the standard error of

---

[5] Charles Spearman, "Coefficient of Correlation Calculated from Faulty Data," *British Journal of Psychology,* 3 (1910), pp. 271–95. In modified form the Spearman-Brown "Prophesy Formula" is:

$$r_{xx} = \frac{2\,r_{oe}}{1 + r_{oe}}$$

where

r_{xx} = coefficient of internal consistency.
r_{oe} = coefficient of correlation between the odd-half scores and the even-half scores.

[6] G. Frederic Kuder and M. W. Richardson, "The Theory of Estimation of Test Reliability," *Psychometrika,* 2 (1937), pp. 151–60.

[7] The formula for the Standard Error of Measurement is as follows:

$$S.E._{m} = \sigma\sqrt{1 - r}$$

where

$S.E._{m}$ = standard error of measurement.
σ = standard deviation of total test scores.
r = coefficient of reliability.

measurement; conversely, the smaller the coefficient of reliability, the larger the standard error of measurement.

To interpret a standard error of measurement, one must differentiate between a student's obtained score and his "true score." The obtained score is the score which the student actually receives when his correct responses have been tabulated, whereas the "true score" is the score which he would have received had the test been totally reliable. Unfortunately, the standard error of measurement does not reveal the size of the difference between a specific obtained score and its "true score." Instead, it allows a statement to be made concerning the size of the difference between obtained scores and "true scores" as it probably exists. Thus, the "true scores" do not differ from their respective obtained scores by more than the size of the standard error of measurement in approximately two-thirds of the measurements which are made with the test in question. Therefore, in the case of one-third of the measurements, the size of the difference exceeds the size of the standard error of measurement. As the size of the standard error of measurement decreases, the obtained scores become better estimates of the "true scores."

Determining Degrees of Validity

Determining the degree of validity of a test is a more complex activity than determining the degree of the test's reliability. Ideally there should be as many determinations of the degree of validity as there are important uses of the test. These uses can be classified into four major categories:[8]

1. The test scores can be interpreted in terms of the student's ability to perform today with respect to a well-defined type of situation or subject matter.
2. The test scores can be used to predict future student behavior.
3. The test scores represent student characteristics not directly measured by the test.
4. The test scores can be interpreted in terms of psychological theory, that is, the test scores have meaning, psychologically speaking.

These four categories lead us to four major types of validity and hence to four major validity determinations. The types of validity

[8] Supplement to the *Psychological Bulletin,* 51, Part 2 (March 1954), pp. 13–28.

are content, predictive, concurrent, and construct. These are listed in the same order as the categories to which they refer.

Content validity. In reality we have already considered the foundation on which the determination of content validity is based. A test possesses content validity to the degree that it adequately samples a defined type of situation or subject matter. In other words, the problem is one of sampling. In the area of achievement testing, this sample problem is guided and controlled by the table of specifications which attempts to reflect the relative importance of the various subcategories of subject matter and the various subcategories of student behavioral changes. For an achievement test to have adequate content validity, it must be composed of test items which in total adequately reflect the relative importance of the cells composing the table of specifications. This table, in turn, must adequately reflect the relative importance of the educational objectives upon which it is based.

Well-developed informal achievement tests quite often have a high degree of content validity. One of the outstanding criticisms of standardized achievement tests is that the degree of their content validity is oftentimes unknown. Moreover, it varies from class to class and from school to school. Unless a teacher has access to the table or tables of specifications or to their equivalent upon which the standardized achievement test was developed, he is in no position to decide whether or not the test possesses adequate content validity for his purposes. In some instances, a definite effort is made to assist the teacher in making this decision. For example, in the case of the Sequential Tests of Educational Progress, a teacher's guide is available, in which detailed breakdowns of the various tests in the battery are shown.[9] These breakdowns reveal the type of subject matter and the type of skill involved in each test item. The breakdowns serve admirably as aids in determining the degree to which a given test in the test battery possesses adequate content validity for a particular teaching situation.

Predictive validity. Predicting future behavior is a most common purpose of testing. The entire area of aptitude testing is based on this purpose. Just as achievement tests must possess a high degree of content validity in order to be useful, so must aptitude tests

[9] Cooperative Test Division, *Sequential Tests of Educational Progress Teacher's Guide* (Princeton, N.J.: Educational Testing Service, 1959).

possess a high degree of predictive validity in order to serve their primary function.

An important illustration of the importance of a high degree of predictive validity can be found in the case of the scholastic aptitude test. For instance, high school seniors are administered scholastic aptitude tests for the purpose of determining, insofar as possible, the likelihood that the seniors will succeed academically in college and university work. These predictions do not need to be totally accurate to be useful. If academic success in college is defined in terms of achievement test scores or in terms of final marks obtained in college, then a criterion is established which can be used as a basis for determining the degree to which the scholastic aptitude tests possess predictive validity.

A longitudinal study of groups of high school seniors who have been administered a scholastic aptitude test can be conducted. Their progress in college is followed and the tabulations of their grade-point averages are made. Scatter diagrams can be plotted, and, as in the case of reliability determinations, a coefficient of correlation can be computed. In such case, the coefficient of correlation is a coefficient of predictive validity; and the larger it is, the greater the degree of predictive validity, insofar as final marks at the college or university in question are concerned.

Coefficients of predictive validity are noticeably smaller in size than the coefficients of reliability. Rarely do they exceed + 0.65. This means that the accuracy of prediction is not nearly as great as it ideally should be. In the case of a given prediction, it is possible to be in error to an alarming degree. However, it must be remembered that predictions based upon psychological tests are viewed as actuarial in nature. Although an individual prediction may be wrong by a sizeable degree, group predictions are generally as accurate as the need requires. In short, it resembles the longevity predictions made by insurance companies. Although they can predict with considerable accuracy the percent of the fifty-year-old men who will live to the age of seventy years, they cannot identify with confidence those individuals who will fail to reach this age and those who will exceed the age mentioned. So it is with predictions based upon psychological tests as well.

The degree to which a test possesses predictive validity is not always represented by a coefficient of correlation. A technique which teachers and counselors find useful and interpretable is that involving expectancy tables.[10]

TABLE 3

EXPECTANCY TABLE FOR SCHOLASTIC APTITUDE AND ACHIEVEMENT TEST SCORES

SCHOLASTIC APTITUDE SCORES	ACHIEVEMENT TEST SCORES			
	Below Average	*Average*	*Above Average*	*Total*
Above Average	0	2	4	6
Average	3	9	3	15
Below Average	5	4	0	9
Total	8	15	7	30

Expectancy tables are in reality a summary of the scatter diagram based upon scholastic aptitude scores and final marks. The expectancy table, like the scatter diagram, is composed of two axes, one representing achievement and one representing aptitude. Achievement is classified into subgroups, for example, above average, average, and below average, and the same is done for aptitude (see Table 3). The number of students in each cell is tabulated. If the scholastic aptitude test possesses a high degree of predictive validity, one would find that students with below average scholastic aptitude have, for the most part, below average academic achievement. Correspondingly, students who have average scholastic aptitude would have average achievement, and those who have above average scholastic aptitude would have above average academic achievement. This relatively simple nine-cell table possesses considerable utility, since it provides a succinct picture of the degree to which the scholastic aptitude test possesses predictive validity when the prediction is to be based upon relatively crude categories instead of specific test scores.

Concurrent validity. Concurrent validity differs from predictive validity only in the sense that it involves a different time element. Whereas predictive validity is an attempt to estimate future performance of the student, concurrent validity is an attempt to

[10] H. R. Kaczkowski, "Using Expectancy Tables to Validate Test Procedures in High School," *Educational and Psychological Measurement,* 19 (Winter 1959), pp. 675–76; and C. H. Lawshe and R. A. Bolda, "Expectancy Charts: I. Their Use and Empirical Development," *Personnel Psychology,* 11 (1958), pp. 353–65.

measure his present performance. This means that the test scores are not a direct reflection of the student performance in question. Instead, they are indirect measurements just as the mercury thermometer is an indirect measurement of the amount of heat in the atmosphere. Measurements of this kind are acceptable, provided that there is a strong relationship between the student characteristic which is observed and the student characteristic which is being estimated.

Concurrent validity plays an important role in achievement testing. For example, a language test which involves vocabulary and word usage can be administered to students for the purpose of estimating these student characteristics as they exist in the everyday activities engaged in by the students. If the test has a high degree of concurrent validity, students with high scores on the test display in their speech and in their informal writing a superior vocabulary and appropriate word usage. Students with lower test scores are correspondingly less able to perform satisfactorily in these respects. Note that the language usage and vocabulary tests do not directly measure the student characteristics to be studied. It undoubtedly is true that test performance is not a totally accurate basis for measuring speech and informal writing practices outside the classroom. To the degree that the test fails to estimate accurately the present student characteristics with regard to speech and informal writing, it lacks concurrent validity. If the lack of concurrent validity is not serious, the use of the test is appropriate since it is an extremely convenient and inexpensive means of determining the nature of student characteristics which would otherwise be unknown because direct observation of student behavior would be difficult.

Construct validity. Construct validity is the most complex of the four types of validity. It lacks the practical flavor of content, predictive, and concurrent validity since it is based upon theoretical considerations. Probably for this reason, there is noticeable controversy concerning the exact nature and importance of construct validity.[11] The issues surrounding construct validity are not likely

---

[11] Jane Loevinger, "Objective Tests as Instruments of Psychological Theory," *Monograph Supplement No. 9, Psychological Reports No. 3* (1957), pp. 635–94; and Lee J. Cronbach and Paul E. Meehl, "Construct Validity in Psychological Tests," *Psychological Bulletin,* 52 (July 1955), pp. 281–302; and H. P. Bechtoldt, "Construct Validity: A Critique," *The American Psychologist,* 14 (October 1959), pp. 619–29.

to be resolved in the immediate future although some attempts have been made to do so.[12]

In essence, construct validity is concerned with the psychological interpretation of test scores.[13] In the case of predictive validity, we are interested only in the ability of test scores to predict future student behavior and are only incidentally concerned as to the interpretation, psychologically speaking, of the aptitude score. Essentially the same is true in the case of concurrent validity. More interest is displayed in the size of the score and its tendency to increase or decrease than is paid to the true psychological meaning of the score. On the other hand, construct validity concerns itself with a relatively broad interpretation of a test score, which in turn means that psychological theory is involved.

Before it can be decided that a test satisfactorily measures a student trait such as general mental ability, one must knew the definition of general mental ability as formulated by those who constructed the test. Should two individuals differ in terms of their definition of this student trait, it is most unlikely that they would agree in their evaluation of the success to which the test reflects the student trait. It is clear that construct validity determination attempts to put meaning behind scores by the use of carefully defined terms.

The study of construct validity is designed on the basis of the theory which was used in the development of the test. In other words, theoretical considerations concerning the nature of general mental ability, for example, would be used to build a test which, it is hoped, is consistent with the theory. If it is consistent, it should yield results which support predictions made on the basis of the theory. Should the predictions made and the test scores yielded by the test concur to a large extent, then evidence is available which supports the contention that the test possesses a high degree of construct validity. If they do not concur, then we are faced with the question of whether the test fails to possess a suitable degree of construct validity or whether the theory is not sound.

---

[12] Donald T. Campbell, "Recommendations for American Psychological Association Test Standards Regarding Construct, Trait, or Discriminant Validity," *American Psychologist,* 15 (August 1960), pp. 546–53.

[13] Lee J. Cronbach, *Essentials of Psychological Testing,* 2nd ed. (New York: Harper & Brothers, Publishers, 1960), p. 106.

The methods used to determine the degree to which a test possesses construct validity are variable. Any technique suitable for testing the hypothesis which is derived from the theoretical argument is suitable for the construct validity determination. This means that, among other techniques, the coefficient of correlation, such as that used in predictive validity, is on occasion suitable for construct validity estimation. In summary, the process of determining the degree to which a test possesses construct validity is much more complex than that for other types of validity.

Establishing Norms

The inability to interpret measurement data adequately becomes quite apparent when examining unfamiliar data. For example, is a 2000-pound automobile a relatively small automobile, an average size automobile, or a relatively large automobile? Or, is a healthy teen-ager who travels one mile on foot in ten minutes walking, running slowly, or running at a great speed? These two questions may be difficult to answer if one is unfamiliar with weights of automobiles and foot race records. The measurements in question are very reliable and valid, but the interpretation of the measurement data is still somewhat obscure. This problem can be corrected by identifying norms, that is, tables of numbers which represent relative performance on the part of reasonably typical individuals.

Norms are based on raw scores and raw scores are the immediate end product of scoring a test, in many cases the number of correct responses made by the student. A raw score of 59 on an algebra achievement test lacks meaning if there is no additional information provided about the student, the test itself, the course of study on which it is based, and the performance of other students in the class. Such a raw score may be the highest of all raw scores in a given group, or it may be about average, or it could be the lowest score. Information concerning the raw scores of other students is needed before the relative position of a raw score of 59 can be found.

A simple and convenient way of beginning the study of the relative position of any particular raw score is to construct a frequency distribution of a group of raw scores within which the one in question occurs. To build a frequency distribution, one subdivides the total spread of the raw scores into a convenient number of intervals of equal size. The raw scores occurring within each interval are tallied and the total frequency is reported. Such a frequency distribution is shown in Table 4. Note the tendency of the algebra raw scores to be clustered near the center of the distribution. At either extreme there are relatively few scores. On the basis of this casual inspection, it is anticipated that the distribution of raw scores may very well be approximately normal, that is, a bell-shaped or gaussian distribution.

TABLE 4

FREQUENCY DISTRIBUTION OF ALGEBRA SCORES

Raw-Score Interval	*Frequency (Number of Students)*
90–94	5
85–89	7
80–84	8
75–79	10
70–74	14
65–69	20
60–64	16
55–59	12
50–54	5
45–49	3
40–44	3
Total	103

Inspection of the frequency distribution reveals that a raw score of 59 falls in the fourth interval from the bottom. A student with such a raw score is definitely in the lower half of the group, but still well above the lowest raw score.

The foregoing identification of relative performance on the part of the student is crude. A number of techniques have been developed which allow much more specific statements to be made about a student's relative performance. Outstanding among these are percentiles and percentile ranks, standard scores, and grade equivalents. Each of these has as its major goal the improvement of the interpretation of the relative performance of a student, yet each attempts to accomplish this task by a different means.

Percentiles and percentile ranks. Percentiles are points in a distribution of test scores, below which fall certain percentages of the test scores. There are 99 such points which divide the total distribution of test scores into 100 equal parts in terms of the number of test scores. The first percentile, known as P_1, is the point below which one per cent of the test scores fall. The second percentile, P_2, is the point below which two per cent of the test scores fall. It follows that the ninety-ninth percentile is known as P_{99} and is the point below which ninety-nine per cent of the test scores fall.

Some of the percentiles are known by other names. For instance, P_{25}, P_{50}, and P_{75} are known as the first quartile (Q_1) and the median (Mdn.) and the third quartile (Q_3), respectively. Also, P_{10}, P_{20}, P_{30}, etc., are known respectively as the first decile (D_1), the second decile (D_2), and the third decile (D_3), etc.

To improve the ease with which percentiles can be used, they are varied slightly. This variation produces the percentile rank. Any raw score of the same size as P_1 or less is identified as the first percentile rank ($P\,R_1$). It follows that any test score larger than P_1 but no larger than P_2 is in the second percentile rank ($P\,R_2$). This continues until P_{99} is reached. Any test score larger than this value is a part of the one hundredth percentile rank ($P\,R_{100}$). In this manner one hundred ranks are established.

Many standardized achievement and aptitude tests contain tables of norms based upon the percentile rank idea. The tables consist of two columns. The first is a list of raw scores. Opposite each is the percentile rank. To interpret a student's raw score, its position in the raw score column is located and the percentile rank which corresponds to it is noted. It can then be said that the student ranks at a certain position (the percentile rank) from the bottom of a standard group of one hundred students who were administered the test. The computation of such a table of percentile ranks is shown in many of the available books devoted to statistical methodology.[14]

Standard scores. Standard score norms are, in essence, norms determined by converting the arithmetic mean (that is, the average) and standard deviation (a measure of score variability) of the raw score distribution to values of a convenient size. The common ancestor of the many standard score systems which have been de-

[14] James E. Wert, Charles O. Neidt, and J. Stanley Ahmann, *Statistical Methods in Educational and Psychological Research* (New York: Appleton-Century-Crofts, Inc., 1954), pp. 46–48.

veloped is the z-score.[15] The z-score is of such a nature that the arithmetic mean of its distribution is always zero and its standard deviation is unity. Hence, any z-score which is negative represents achievement which is below the arithmetic mean, whereas any z-score which is positive represents success in terms of the test which exceeds the arithmetic mean. For all practical purposes, the largest z-score is + 3.00 and the smallest is − 3.00.

A much more popular standard score than the z-score is the stanine score.[16] The stanine scale is a nine-point scale of standard scores with an arithmetic mean of five and a standard deviation of two. The scores generally vary from a low of one to a high of nine. As in the case of the z-score, these reference points are easily memorized and interpretation of relative performance of a student is facilitated.

Perhaps the most popular of the standard score is that which is sometimes known as the T-score.[17] A distribution of T-scores has an arithmetic mean of 50 and a standard deviation of 10. The practical limits of this distribution are 80 and 20.

The pattern of the standard-score distributions is now becoming evident. In addition to the three mentioned, there is a standard score with an arithmetic mean of 100 and a standard deviation of 20 with a practical high of 160 and a practical low of 40. This standard score is used with the Army General Classification Test (AGCT), which has been widely administered. If the arithmetic mean is raised to 500 and the standard deviation to 100, the practical high of the distribution becomes 800 and the practical low 200. In this case,

---

[15] The formula for the z-score is as follows:

$$z = \frac{X - M}{\sigma}$$

where

z = standard score.
X = any raw score of a given distribution.
M = arithmetic means of the raw-score distribution.
σ = standard deviation of the raw-score distribution.

[16] Walter N. Durost, "The Characteristics, Use, and Computation of Stanines," *Test Service Notebook*, No. 23 (New York: World Book Company, 1959).

[17] The formula for the T-score is as follows:

$$T = 10\,(z) + 50$$

where

T = standard score.
z = z-score for the raw score in question.

the standard score is that which is used to represent a student's success when he is administered the Scholastic Aptitude Tests of the College Entrance Examination Board (CEEB).

The interrelationships among the standard scores described and percentiles are shown in a succinct fashion in Figure 2.[18] Notice that these relationships are based upon the very important assumption that the raw-score distribution is a normal one. To the degree

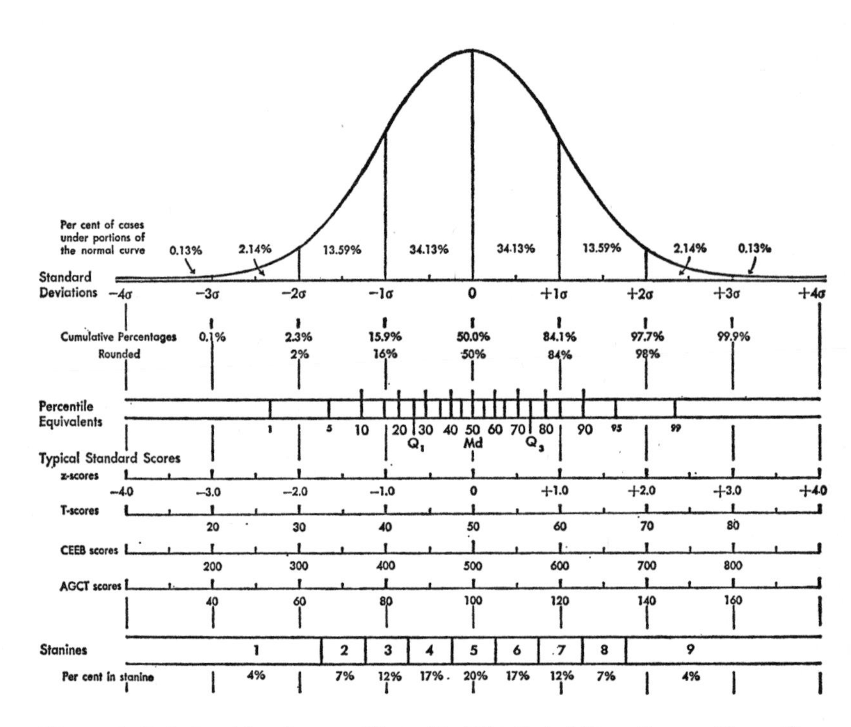

Figure 2. Relationships Among Normally Distributed Raw Scores, Percentiles, and Certain Standard Scores.

that this assumption is not appropriate, the utility of Figure 2 diminishes. In the case of unselected groups of students (that is, students who are unselected in terms of the characteristic being measured by a test), the distribution of raw scores strongly resembles the normal curve in most cases. However, even in these

[18] Harold G. Seashore, "Methods of Expressing Test Scores," *Test Service Bulletin,* No. 48 (New York: The Psychological Corporation, 1955).

instances the assumption that a normal curve exists should not be made blindly. Statistical techniques are available which provide evidence on the basis of which a distribution of raw scores can be identified, for all practical purposes, as a normal distribution or not a normal distribution. Evidence concerning the degree to which a specific distribution of raw scores approaches the normal distribution should be examined before comparisons, such as those suggested in Figure 2, are made.

Grade equivalents. Although percentile ranks and standard scores are a very common means of representing relative performance of students in high schools and colleges, probably the most widely used means of representing relative performance of elementary school students is the grade equivalent. The grade equivalent for any raw score is the grade level of those students whose average raw score is the same as the raw score in question. In other words, if the average raw score happened to be 71 in the case of a test administered to fifth-grade students in late September, the raw score of 71 has a grade equivalent of 5.0.

Grade equivalents are designated by two numbers, the first of which represents the year (in terms of grade level) and the second of which represents the month. The calendar year is divided into ten parts, nine representing the academic year and one representing the summer months.

Unless the grade equivalent of a student represents extremely low success or extremely high success in terms of a test, they are very easy to interpret. One simply compares the student's actual grade level with the grade equivalents he obtains on any test which is administered to him. If the grade equivalents noticeably surpass his present grade level, he has succeeded better than the average student. On the other hand, if his grade equivalent is essentially the same as his grade level, he is succeeding in an average fashion. Finally, if his grade equivalent is noticeably lower than his grade level, he is not succeeding as well as his classmates.

Interpretation of norms. Although the use of norms facilitates the ease with which the relative performance of a student can be identified, there are still two major problems with regard to the interpretation of norms which are sometimes overlooked. The first of these problems stems from the fact that the uninitiated teacher, student, or parent overinterprets the accuracy of the norm. They somehow gain the impression that, because the raw score has been converted to a standard score or percentile rank, the representation of student performance is much more accurate. The second problem concerns the standardization or norm group on the basis of which the tables of norms were developed. Notice in Table 4 that a relatively large group of students is involved in the first steps of determining a specific student's relative performance. This is true of all of the techniques mentioned in the foregoing discussion. Needless to say, the nature of this group is very important when one attempts to interpret with care the relative performance of a student. After all, his performance is relative to that group. It must be reasonable to compare him with the members of the group.

Accuracy of norms. The unreliability of each test demands that each raw score, or any norm derived on the basis of it, be viewed as a region or band rather than as a single point as it seems to be. This region or band is relatively small when the reliability of the test is extremely high, that is, when the standard error of measurement is extremely small. It follows that the region or band increases in size as the reliability of the test decreases, or as the standard error of measurement becomes larger. A common way of determining the size of the band is to add the standard error of measurement to the test score to find the upper limit of the band, and to subtract it from the test score to find the lower limit of the band. When this is done, the following interpretation is made: "The chances are about two to one that the student's 'true score' falls somewhere within this band." Although this interpretation is not entirely appropriate, it does represent the intent of the band approach. Naturally the band could be enlarged so that the odds are increased, but this does not happen in many instances.

The use of bands is becoming popular in the case of standardized achievement and aptitude tests.[19] Test batteries including a series of achievement tests and, possibly, several scholastic aptitude tests produce profiles of student success. Each bar of the profile represents a student characteristic. The student's success with regard to the test based on this characteristic is represented by a band. If any two bands overlap to any degree, it is highly unlikely that the

---

[19] Score Bands are used to interpret test results from the School and College Ability Tests and the Sequential Tests of Educational Progress published by the Cooperative Test Division of the Educational Testing Service.

student differs in terms of his relative success in the two areas in question. Should two bands not overlap, then it is highly likely that he does indeed differ with regard to the characteristics in question. In the latter instances the odds may exceed five to one that a true difference in student success is present.

It is clear that small differences in test scores and, therefore, in norms are equally meaningless. The bands computed would overlap to a considerable extent, and the student very likely would not display a true difference in terms of the two characteristics represented by the two test scores. Only large differences between norm values are considered to be true differences, therefore requiring interpretation and, possibly, some action on the part of teacher, counselor, or administrator.

Standardization groups. The problem of selecting the proper sample for determining test norms is far more difficult than commonly supposed. If there is reason to believe that students from small high schools differ from students from large high schools, that male students differ from female students, or that students from one geographic area differ from those from other areas in terms of the characteristic measured by a test, then it follows that separate samples should be drawn from each group. If only one sample is used, it should be stratified according to the characteristics which cause the population to be heterogeneous in terms of the student characteristic being measured by the test.

More and more standardized tests have not one, but a series of tables of norms, each table representing a reasonably homogeneous subgroup of students for whom the test is designed. Determining a student's relative performance means that the teacher must select the most appropriate table of norms and then identify the student's relative performance in terms of the standardization group used in the case of that table. A brief description of the standardization group must be given in order to make possible an appropriate interpretation of the student's relative performance.

The Mental Measurements Yearbooks

Determinations of reliability and validity, as well as the establishment of norms, are very much a private matter in the case of informal tests. Typically, no systematic attempt is made to find definitive evidence concerning validity and reliability, and only limited attempts are made to identify relative performance. This is not true in the case of standardized achievement and aptitude tests. Today elaborate steps are taken to present evidence on the basis of which one can evaluate the degree to which the instrument is reliable and valid, and the test authors and publishers spend much time and energy in the production of a series of tables of norms in order to provide a convenient basis for interpreting the relative performance of almost any student to whom the test may be administered.

Examining and evaluating the mass of information provided in the case of the modern achievement and standardized tests is not a small task. Some users of tests find that they are either incapable of properly appraising this material, or they lack the time in which to accomplish such a task. Consequently, they rely on a highly useful series of yearbooks which contain information that helps them make decisions concerning the utility of a particular test. The yearbooks are the *Mental Measurements Yearbooks,* the first volume of which was published in 1938. Since that date, additional volumes have been published at regular intervals.

The most useful part of each of the yearbooks is that part known as "Tests and Reviews." Here are reports concerning the validity, reliability, and norms of the test in question. The reviews of the tests are in most instances extremely frank. When more than one review is available, they are sometimes contradictory. In addition, a series of pertinent bibliographical references is included.

The most recent yearbook is the *Fifth Mental Measurements Yearbook*[20] which, although it is extremely large, supplements, rather than supplants, the preceding four volumes. It contains 957 evaluation instrument titles, 698 original reviews, and 6,468 references. Teachers, counselors, supervisors, and school administrators, as well as admissions officers and research workers, find this yearbook and its four predecessors to be of unusual value when they wish to determine the utility of a particular standardized achievement or aptitude test.

---

[20] Oscar K. Buros, ed., *The Fifth Mental Measurements Yearbook* (Highland Park, N.J.: The Gryphon Press, 1959).

CHAPTER IV

Testing in the Cognitive Domain

The scope of the cognitive domain is indeed striking. Even the most casual inspection clearly reveals the wide variations which exist within this domain. If one observes the small child who finds pleasure in being able to name the continents of the world or recite the alphabet, and if one listens to a debate between skilled political scientists concerning the goals and programs of the United States in this decade, he will probably be alternately impressed and confused by the depth of the vocabulary applied and the subtleness of the ideas which are manipulated. Both of these extremes fall within the cognitive domain and neither represents the greatest degree of either extreme which exists. Thus, the cognitive domain includes the most simple and the most complex of the intellectual abilities and skills possessed by man.

The platform on which the cognitive domain is developed is knowledge. The individual must be able to recall at will necessary information before he can acquire higher-order intellectual skills. It is not surprising, therefore, that many educational objectives and many evaluation attempts are directed toward knowledge and the degree to which the student has acquired it. It would be a serious mistake if the educational objectives and the evaluation attempts based upon them did not also attempt to determine the degree to which students have acquired higher-order levels of intellectual ability. Educational objectives are spread throughout the cognitive domain and the evaluation techniques used in connection with them must be extremely versatile.

There is little doubt that the evaluation techniques typically used by the classroom teacher fail to represent the many variations of student development which occur in the cognitive domain. There is an overemphasis on the evaluation of knowledge. Although there is a reasonably high degree of relationship between the extent to which students acquire knowledge and the extent to which they acquire higher-order intellectual skills, the relationship is still sufficiently imperfect that any teacher whose evaluation program is primarily based on knowledge cannot safely generalize, on the basis of that information, the degree to which the student has acquired the higher-order skills. The nature of this problem becomes vividly apparent when one observes some of the almost comical attempts on the part of students to apply information which, in terms of tests of knowledge at least, they seem to command. For example, one student clearly revealed the true extent of his command of the material which he was studying when he proudly announced to his mother: "Today we studied jubilant delinquency!" His difficulties are probably no greater than another student who informed his teacher that he missed a great deal of school last year because he had "indolent fever."[1]

These are but two of a near infinite number of humorous instances when embarrassing "boners" are detected. Needless to say, we tend to be tolerant of them and oftentimes suspect that our ear rather than the speaker has failed us. However, there is no room for such doubt when, as happened in the case of the New York State Regents Examinations a few years ago, a teacher scoring one of the tests discovered that a student identified Eugene O'Neill as "a winner of the Bullet Surprise." No doubt this teacher speculated for a considerable length of time with respect to the reasons for this most unusual response and the implications of it with regard to his teaching and evaluating procedures.

Bloom and his co-workers[2] attempted to clarify the cognitive domain by subdividing it into six categories: knowledge, comprehension, application, analysis, synthesis, and evaluation. From the point of view of testing, the knowledge category offers the least amount of difficulty (see Chapter II). On the other hand, the remaining five categories, which are sometimes known as the realm of understanding, are relatively undeveloped insofar as informal and, to some degree, standardized achievement testing is concerned. In an effort to improve the situation, Bloom not only classified objectives into the five categories but also listed essay and objective test items which would be suitable for evaluating student behavior in terms of the various categories of understanding.

---

[1] Edgar Dale, "How to Improve Your Vocabulary," *The Bureau of Educational Research Newsletter,* 23 (April 1958), p. 4.

[2] Benjamin S. Bloom, *Taxonomy of Educational Objectives* (New York: Longmans, Green & Company, Inc., 1956), pp. 201–7.

Measuring Understandings

Measuring the degree to which students possess understandings is not an easy task and certainly cannot be accomplished by one technique alone. Since understandings are complex, we expect that the manifestations of them are also complex. This means, in turn, that a variety of evaluation instruments are needed in order to determine within any degree of accuracy the extent to which the student possesses a particular understanding. The analysis of student procedures and products is certainly appropriate here. This means that nontest evaluation procedures can serve well in this respect.

Insofar as paper-and-pencil instruments are concerned, the essay test plays an important role. Even when the student response to an essay test item is relatively restricted, it still represents, in some respects at least, the student's abilities to be creative, his ability to organize his thinking, and his ability to communicate effectively. On the other hand, the objective test has not enjoyed the popularity of the essay test when student understandings are to be measured, although there is good reason to believe that the objective test is capable of measuring student understandings in an efficient fashion. The versatility of the objective test is no doubt underestimated. As a result, many informal achievement tests and some standardized achievement tests measure little more than the student's command of knowledge.

It must be remembered that it is most difficult to classify objective test items in terms of the category in the taxonomy with which they are most closely related. The mental processes used to solve the test item are obviously important. Also, the past experiences of the student—in particular, his recent learning experiences—determine whether a given test item requires him to do more than recall information. A number of modern standardized achievement tests are using test items that measure more than the student's ability to recall information. Also, attempts have been made to design objective test items for measuring understanding in a wide variety of subject-matter areas.[3] The results of these efforts are highly encouraging.

---

[3] Nelson B. Henry, ed., *The Measurement of Understanding,* Forty-Fifth Yearbook of the National Society for the Study of Education, Part I (Chicago, Illinois: The University of Chicago Press, 1946); and Floyd Monaghan, "Design of Objective Test Items to Evaluate Thinking Ability in Science," *Science Education,* 44 (December 1960), pp. 358–66.

Course-Oriented Standardized Achievement Tests

Hundreds of standardized achievement tests are available today. The content of such tests is typically based upon a detailed study of commonly used textbooks, reference books, and study guides. In this way it is hoped that a high degree of content validity is present in each of these course-oriented achievement tests. Such tests are then standardized on large groups of students who are thought to be representative of a population of students for whom the test is designed.

Course-oriented standardized achievement tests should be used and interpreted with some degree of care. No achievement test can be all things to all teachers and students, yet some advertising literature and test salesmen would lead one to believe that the products they are promoting are capable of this high degree of versatility. Well-developed, informal achievement tests have a noticeably higher degree of content validity than most of the corresponding standardized tests when they are used to determine the degree to which the student can recall information. In the realm of testing for student understanding, the superiority of the informal achievement test is not well-established.

The complexity of the item construction problem prevents the classroom teacher from engaging seriously in this type of paper-and-pencil testing. Instead, he turns to the standardized achievement test which is the product of the work of professionals. Nevertheless, the use of such an instrument is inappropriate unless there is satisfactory evidence of a suitable degree of content validity. In other words, the kinds of student behavioral changes and subject-matter areas which the teacher has in mind are very similar to those which the professional test builder has in mind. The needed evidence can be obtained by comparing teacher-designed tables of specifications with those sometimes provided by the publishers of course-oriented standardized achievement tests and by a careful follow-up study of the content of the standardized test itself. Indeed, it is even profitable for the teacher to administer the test to himself before he decides to administer it to the students under his direction.

The course-oriented standardized achievement tests now available cover every conceivable subject-matter area and, with certain important exceptions, almost all class levels. Only in the sophomore, junior, and senior years of college does one find relatively few course-oriented standardized achievement tests. In many respects the most successful standardized achievement tests are in the area of the basic skills, particularly in the areas of reading and mathematics in the elementary school. Commonness of educational objectives plus the unquestioned importance of these areas has stimulated the development and improvement of achievement tests here.

Representative of the numerous course-oriented achievement tests currently available are the Cooperative Achievement Tests published by the Cooperative Test Division of the Educational Testing Service, and the Evaluation and Adjustment Series published by Harcourt, Brace & World, Inc. The former are designed to measure the educational achievement of students enrolled in academic subject-matter areas in the junior high school, senior high school, and college, whereas the latter is a series of tests for the secondary schools only. The reliability of these tests is for the most part quite good. The degree of content validity must be determined by the teacher who wishes to use the test, and he must do so in terms of the students and teaching situation with which he is confronted.

Many course-oriented achievement tests, such as the Cooperative Biology Test and the Cooperative Chemistry Test for high school students, contain both test items which are designed to measure knowledge of terms and concepts and test items which are designed to measure the student's ability to apply his knowledge in new situations. As a result, the Cooperative Test Division claims that the test results reveal areas of relative strength and weakness concerning the student's academic achievement. This, in turn, allows for more satisfactory placement of that student and better uniformity of admission and promotion standards.

Standardized Achievement Test Batteries

The standardized achievement test batteries cover many, or all, of the principal subject-matter areas mentioned in the foregoing paragraphs. Because the tests are developed by a single team or coordinated teams of testing and subject-matter specialists, and because they are standardized on the same samples of students, profiles of the student's achievement can be plotted and interpreted with relative ease. These profiles present a picture of the student's relative strengths and weaknesses insofar as achievement in academic subject-matter areas is concerned. By comparing the scores which the student made on the various subtests which composed the test battery, the tester can decide whether a given student has any outstanding variations in the pattern of his achievement.

Achievement test batteries have been prepared for the elementary school level, the secondary school level, and for all class levels from kindergarten through the fourteenth level. For the most part, these batteries have been built with considerable care and are outstandingly successful in providing information for longitudinal studies of student achievement in a given school system. Moreover, they usually have a healthy balance between test items which primarily measure recall of information and test items which measure student understandings. Indeed, some test batteries are devoted primarily to the second of the two categories. The test authors argue that educational personnel are, above all, interested in the more complex and more lasting outcomes of the educational process, that is, in the realm of student understandings. Moreover, student knowledges, they argue, can be measured to a satisfactory degree by the well-developed informal test and, hence, need not be an important concern of standardized achievement tests.

Elementary school test batteries. Of the many achievement test batteries prepared for the elementary school, three have received considerable attention. These are the Iowa Tests of Basic Skills,[4] the Metropolitan Achievement Tests,[5] and the Stanford Achievement Test.[6] As the name suggests, the Iowa Tests of Basic Skills are concerned exclusively with the fundamentals of instruction in the elementary school, that is, the three R's. In each test the student is required to use a basic skill in much the same manner as he would in the classroom or outside of it. Fifteen scores spread over five major areas are available for each student. The areas and their subparts are as follows:

---

[4] Published by the Houghton Mifflin Company, New York, 1955.
[5] Published by Harcourt, Brace & World, Inc., New York, 1959.
[6] Published by Harcourt, Brace & World, Inc., New York, 1953.

- Vocabulary
- Reading Comprehension
- Language Skills
    - Spelling
    - Capitalization
    - Punctuation
    - Usage
- Work-Study Skills
    - Map Reading
    - Reading Graphs and Tables
    - Knowledge and Use of Reference Materials
- Arithmetic Skills
    - Arithmetic Concepts
    - Arithmetic Problem Solving

The Metropolitan Achievement Tests are composed of five batteries: Primary I, Primary II, Elementary, Intermediate, and Advanced. The scope of the batteries varies in that the Primary I, Primary II, and Elementary batteries emphasize basic skills only, whereas the Intermediate and Advanced batteries include the subject-matter areas of social studies and science. In the case of the Intermediate and Advanced batteries, which are the most complete of the five batteries, the following areas are included:

- Word Knowledge
- Reading
- Arithmetic Computation
    - Arithmetic Concepts
- Arithmetic Problem Solving
- Spelling
- Language
- Language Study Skills
- Social Studies Information
- Social Studies Study Skills
- Science

In the case of the Stanford Achievement Test, four batteries are available: the Primary battery, the Elementary battery, the Intermediate battery, and the Advanced battery. The Primary battery is relatively short, containing tests in paragraph meaning, word meaning, spelling, arithmetic, reasoning, arithmetic reasoning, and arithmetic computation. The Intermediate battery and the Advanced battery are the longest, yielding ten scores. In the case of these two batteries, the following tests are included:

Paragraph Meaning
Word Meaning
Social Studies (History and Geography)
Science
Language
Arithmetic Reasoning
Arithmetic Computation
Spelling
Study Skills

In Table 5 is a simplified comparison of the three test batteries insofar as the batteries designed for the intermediate class levels (grades 4, 5, and 6) are concerned. Although there is considerable similarity in the scope of the three batteries and in the per cent of total testing time allotted to each area, there are still several outstanding differences among the three test batteries. For example, the Iowa Tests of Basic Skills, as previously noted, do not include subtests in the area of the social studies and science, but devote over one-fourth of the total testing available to the measurement of student study skills. In contrast, the Metropolitan Achievement Tests allot almost twenty per cent of the testing time for measuring student knowledges and understandings in social studies and make no attempt to measure student study skills in general. It should be noted, however, that this test battery contains a subtest concerning social studies study skills and another concerning language study skills.

TABLE 5

PERCENTAGE OF TESTING TIME ALLOTTED VARIOUS AREAS INCLUDED IN THREE ELEMENTARY SCHOOL ACHIEVEMENT TEST BATTERIES

Area	*Iowa Tests of Basic Skills*	*Metropolitan Achievement Tests*	*Stanford Achievement Test*
Reading Comprehension	19.7	10.1	11.7
Vocabulary	6.1	5.7	5.6
Fundamentals of Arithmetic	10.7	16.2	16.4
Arithmetic Reasoning	10.7	15.0	16.4
Language	19.7	20.2	7.5
Spelling	4.3	6.9	7.0
Study Skills	28.7	—	18.8
Science	—	6.9	7.0
Social Studies	—	19.0	9.4

Crude analyses of the elementary school test batteries, such as that shown in Table 5, are useful when selection of a test battery is to be made. It allows the teacher, the student, and his parents to obtain a quick over-view of the scope of the test battery and, as such, sets the stage for a more thorough analysis of the characteristics of the instruments.

Secondary school test batteries. Three popular secondary school achievement test batteries are the Essential High School Content Battery,[7] the California Survey Series,[8] and the Iowa Tests of Educational Development.[9] These three batteries vary considerably from each other as contrasted with the high degree of similarity which exists among the three elementary school achievement test batteries already described. The first of the three is relatively restricted in scope, whereas the remaining two cover a wide variety of areas and require considerable testing time.

The Essential High School Content Battery is composed of four subtests: Mathematics, Science, Social Studies, and English. The tests are heavily oriented toward the recall of information section of the cognitive domain. Hence, the degree of content validity which they contain no doubt varies appreciably from one class to another.

In contrast, the California Survey Series is composed of ten tests which are intended to measure the student's general and specific academic potential plus his educational achievement in the basic skill areas of reading, arithmetic, language, and spelling, and in the subject-matter areas of history, geography, physical science, and biological science. The following areas are included in this series:

- Mental Ability Area
    - Survey of Mental Maturity
- Basic Skills Area
    - Survey of Reading Achievement
    - Survey of Arithmetic (Mathematics) Achievement
    - Survey of Language Achievement
- Science Area
    - Survey Test in Introductory Science
    - Survey Test in Physical Science
    - Survey Test in Biological Science

[7] Published by Harcourt, Brace & World, Inc., New York, 1952.
[8] Published by the California Test Bureau, Los Angeles, 1960.
[9] Published by the Science Research Associates, Inc., Chicago, 1952.

Social Science Area
- Survey Test in Introductory American History
- Survey Test in Geography

Algebra Aptitude
- Survey Test of Algebraic Aptitude

Perhaps the most widely used and most carefully developed of the three achievement test batteries for the secondary school are the Iowa Tests of Educational Development. Nine tests are included in this battery and, interestingly enough, they are not thought of as tests of subject matter as such. It is the intent of the test author to measure the broad intellectual skills and interests of the student as well as his understanding of, and his ability to use, information which has been learned. In short, the purpose of the battery is to measure ability to think critically and to apply factual information, rather than to measure ability to recall information. This battery, then, is designed in terms of the understanding realm of cognitive domain.

The nine tests of the Iowa Tests of Educational Development are:

Understanding of Basic Social Concepts
General Background in the Natural Sciences
Correctness and Appropriateness of Expression
Ability to do Quantitative Thinking
Interpretation of Reading Materials in the Social Studies
Interpretation of Reading Materials in the Natural Sciences
Interpretation of Literary Materials
General Vocabulary
Use of Sources of Information

A sidelight to the utility of the Iowa Tests of Educational Development is their degree of predictive validity.[10] The relationship between students' test scores from this battery and their subsequent academic success in college is appreciable. Consequently, considerable research concerning the predictive validity of this battery has been completed, and teachers and counselors use the profiles of the students for anticipating likely academic success in various fields in higher education.

School-wide achievement test batteries. The advantages of a longitudinal study of a student's achievement pattern are so great

---

[10] Science Research Associates, *Using the Iowa Tests of Educational Development for College Planning* (Chicago, Illinois: Science Research Associates, Inc.).

that much attention has been given to the development and administration of achievement test batteries which are suitable for all class levels from the primary level of the elementary school to the early years in college. Two outstanding illustrations of test batteries designed for this wide usage are the California Achievement Tests (WXYZ Series)[11] and the Sequential Tests of Educational Progress.[12]

Each of these two achievement test batteries is an articulated series of tests which measure at various class levels the degree of student achievement in the same basic learning areas. On the other hand, there are several important differences between the two batteries. For instance, the California Achievement Tests are exclusively objective tests, whereas the Sequential Tests of Educational Progress contain an essay writing test, a type of test rarely found in a standardized achievement test battery.

A more important difference between the California Achievement Tests and the Sequential Tests of Educational Progress is that the former battery is restricted to the measurement of student achievement in the areas of reading, arithmetic, and language skills, whereas the latter is designed to measure student achievement in seven areas: Reading, Writing, Listening, Social Studies, Science, Mathematics, and Essay. Each of these tests is intended to measure the ability of the student to apply his knowledge rather than his command of specific subject matter. Four levels of each test are available. The levels ranging from Level 1, intended for college freshmen and sophomores, to Level 4, intended for grades 4, 5, and 6.

The Sequential Tests of Educational Progress have several unusual features which may prove to be important indicators of the future trends in achievement test batteries. For instance, the mathematics, science, and social studies tests make little or no effort to measure the degree of student knowledge. Instead, they concentrate, insofar as possible, on the higher-order learnings in the cognitive domain. Also, the essay test is somewhat of an innovation. In this test, the student is to write a theme on one of several topics, the theme then being scored in terms of certain designed standards.

---

[11] Published by the California Test Bureau, Los Angeles, 1957.

[12] Published by the Cooperative Test Division of the Educational Testing Service, Princeton, New Jersey, 1957.

Finally, the listening test represents a re-emphasis on a skill of known importance. Passages and questions are read to the student who must then find answers in his test booklet and record his answers on his answer sheet. The essay and listening tests, along with reading and writing tests, represent an effort to measure the effectiveness of the student's communication skills in a broad and intensive manner.

Interpreting Standardized Achievement Test Scores

Not the least of the testing problems confronting the teacher, the student, and his parents is the interpretation of the standardized achievement test score after it has been determined. Even the brief descriptions in the foregoing paragraphs concerning various standardized achievement tests and test batteries reveals that the size of the score alone is only the first piece of evidence needed to evaluate adequately the student's achievement. In addition to knowing the nature of the type of norm used to represent the student's relative performance, the tester must be intimately familiar with the achievement test's content validity and its reliability. The more important of these is, of course, the question of content validity.

Content validity and score interpretation. In the preceding descriptions of various standardized achievement tests, expressions such as "social studies" and "science" are used repeatedly. Exactly what do these expressions mean? One may not be surprised to find that, insofar as test content is concerned, the expression "social studies" means something at least slightly different from one test to another; but it may be quite surprising to discover that this same expression varies in its meaning within an articulated series of tests, such as the Sequential Tests of Educational Development. In the case of this series of tests, social studies includes American history, geography, social anthropology, government, economics, and world history. However, the degree to which each of these subject-matter areas contributes to the test varies from level to level.

This variance is necessary so that the social studies test at a particular level will possess an acceptable degree of content validity for that level. For example, there is a heavy emphasis on American history at all levels. However, it is occasionally as low as approximately one-third and as high as approximately one-half, depending upon the level in question. Geography is even a better illustration of the problem. At the lower levels the emphasis on geography in the social studies test is appreciable—approaching fifty per cent. However, at the upper levels its importance, as expected, drops off greatly; less than twenty per cent of the test items pertain to geography.

The foregoing analysis should not be interpreted as a criticism of the Sequential Tests of Educational Progress. It is clear that the contribution of geography to the social studies tests, for instance, should decrease greatly as one moves from the lower levels to the upper levels. On the other hand, this does change the meaning of the concept "social studies" as applied to these tests. Until we know the precise contribution made by the various subject-matter areas to the total composite known as social studies, we will be unable to interpret test scores yielded by this test. Fortunately, a teacher's guide[13] for the Sequential Tests of Educational Progress is provided to assist in the interpretation of test scores from this test battery. For six of the tests (the essay test is not included) and for each level of each test, a breakdown is provided for all test items within the test with respect to the type of subject matter involved in the test item and the type of student skill which is required in order to answer the test item successfully. Such an item-by-item analysis of a test is invaluable information when an interpretation of an achievement test score is to be made. Test scores must be interpreted in terms of the test items which yielded those scores rather than in terms of test titles which are, at best, vastly oversimplified labels identifying the student characteristic in question.

---

[13] Cooperative Test Division, *Sequential Tests of Educational Progress Teacher's Guide* (Princeton, N.J.: Educational Testing Service, 1959), pp. 19–85.

CHAPTER V

Determining Student Potential

"There is something that is much more scarce, something finer by far, something rarer than ability. It is the ability to recognize ability." Elbert Hubbard, the author of this statement, is speaking of a troubling aspect of one's interpersonal relationships. Each of us informally appraises the abilities of our friends and colleagues. In the world of business and industry important decisions are made on the basis of appraisals of ability, and the success and failure of an enterprise may be determined in large degree by the appropriateness of these decisions.

The situation is no different in formal education. It is necessary for teachers and school administrators to make judgments concerning student potential, particularly academic potential, and to organize teaching programs and to evaluate student success on the basis of these appraisals. Fortunately, as in the case of business and industry, it is not necessary to rely on informal techniques in order to obtain needed information concerning potential. A large variety of reasonably well-developed and standardized instruments are available which are capable of yielding data on the basis of which evaluations can be made of human potential in a wide variety of areas.

In education the scholastic aptitude of a student is clearly the most vital aspect of his total potential. However, one cannot ignore other aptitudes such as mechanical, musical, artistic, clerical, and spatial. Tests are available in all of these areas, but only in the case of scholastic aptitude are they widely administered. The less important areas are of interest to teachers and counselors in the case of only a part of the student body with which they are concerned. Hence, administration of tests in these areas in a wholesale manner is relatively uncommon. Ordinarily, such tests are administered to students only in the case of special need.

Differentiating Between Achievement and Aptitude Tests

An aptitude is an individual's potential for learning a given skill when he is provided with appropriate instruction. The aptitude family of student characteristics is certainly different from his achievements, which are his current status with respect to the skill in question. He can have relatively low achievement and, simultaneously, relatively high aptitude in a given respect.

In terms of aptitude tests and achievement tests, the differentiation is by no means clear. The content of tests in these two areas sometimes is so similar that one is unable to differentiate between aptitude and achievement test items when lifted out of context. This problem stems from the fact that test builders commonly assume that the best way to determine one's potential for a given future skill is to examine his achievement in that area or related areas today. Consequently, some aptitude tests, particularly scholastic aptitude tests, strongly resemble achievement tests. Indeed, the tendency for this to occur seems to become stronger as the years pass.

Scholastic aptitude tests (or general mental ability tests, as they are sometimes called) cover a wide variety of content. This point has been well illustrated by Cronbach.[1] He describes the variability of the test content of general mental ability tests by identifying the degree to which the tests are measures of the outcomes of education. He classifies the degree of educational loading into six categories: (1) Subject-matter proficiency; (2) General educational development; (3) Reading, vocabulary, arithmetic reasoning; (4) Verbal analogies, number series; (5) Figure series, matrices; and (6) Learning samples. The maximum educational loading is, of course, the first category, subject-matter proficiency, whereas the minimum educational loading is the last category, learning samples. Tests which emphasize the first category are ordinary achievement tests devoted to a specific body of subject matter. Tests which emphasize the last two categories deal with tasks which involve concepts and experiences familiar to all examinees but which still challenge the

[1] Lee J. Cronbach, *Essentials of Psychological Testing,* 2nd ed. (New York: Harper & Brothers, Publishers, 1960), p. 235.

reasoning power of that person. In the case of these tests, the emphasis upon language and culture is relatively small.

Many of the mental ability tests used in formal education today cover more than one of the six categories. Usually, they do not emphasize the last two categories. Instead, they concentrate on the middle of the list, that is, on the reading, vocabulary, and arithmetic reasoning category, as well as the verbal analogies and number series category. Several important tests overlap the second category, the general educational development category, and thereby create confusion when one attempts to differentiate between achievement and aptitude tests in terms of test content. In this respect the overlap between an achievement test and a corresponding mental ability test can be very great.[2]

In summary, the achievement tests and aptitude tests used in formal education are identified primarily on the basis of their purpose, rather than on the basis of their test content. The fact that the test content of achievement tests and tests of mental ability tend to overlap a great deal is a less serious matter than often supposed. If the tests in the respective areas serve, to a satisfactory degree, the purposes for which their use is intended, then no serious doubts should exist with regard to their utility.

Individual Tests of Mental Ability

Formal attempts to measure mental ability began with individual testing. The first individual to make important progress in this effort was Alfred Binet, a French physician who became interested in the problem about 1890, and who developed the Binet scale about 20 years later. This scale is an important milestone in the development of formal testing techniques. Lewis M. Terman revised Binet's work and developed the Stanford revision of the Binet scale in 1916. The 1916 edition was revised in 1937 and again in 1960.

Stanford-Binet Intelligence Scale. Like the preceding two editions, the third edition of the Stanford-Binet Intelligence Scale[3] is a widely used instrument, particularly when the mental ability of elementary school children with unusual problems is to be meas-

[2] William Coleman and E. E. Cureton, "Intelligence and Achievement: The 'Jangle Fallacy' Again," *Educational and Psychological Measurement,* 14 (Summer 1954), pp. 347–51.

[3] Published by the Houghton Mifflin Company, New York, 1960.

ured. It consists of one form which can be used to measure the mental ability of school-age individuals, and it must be administered by a qualified examiner to one individual at a time.

The Stanford-Binet is composed of twenty scales, all but one of which contains six items. In total, there are 122 items plus 20 alternate items. In the case of the first seven scales (mental age two to mental age five), each item is equivalent to one month of mental age. In the case of the next nine scales (mental age six to mental age fourteen), each of the six items in the scale is equivalent to two months of mental age. The last four scales, Average Adult, Superior Adult I, Superior Adult II, and Superior Adult III, have eight, six, six, and six items, respectively. The amount of mental age credit per item varies from scale to scale. In the case of the Average Adult scale, it is two months; Superior Adult I, four months; Superior Adult II, five months; and Superior Adult III, six months.

Administration. Like most individual tests, the administration of the Stanford-Binet scale is difficult. The examiner must have considerable experience with the instrument and must be able to administer it in a precise manner and still maintain rapport with the child. The room must be quiet and relatively free of distractions. Normally, no other individuals are present; certainly those who are centers of reference or authority are not present. The administration of the test may require one hour or more. If fatigue seems to bother the child, then the administration is divided into two periods. In any event, the examiner must maintain standard testing conditions.

The administration procedures of the test require that the child start at a level below that which is expected of him. These easy tasks build confidence in the child and establish the basal age, that is, a scale level at which the child successfully passes all of the tests. The testing continues to the higher levels until the child fails all of the tests at a particular level. His success is expressed in terms of months of mental age.

The nature of the response which a child makes when being administered the Stanford-Binet varies considerably. At the lower age scales a number of motor responses are required. For example, the child is required to manipulate beads on a string, to handle blocks, and to place objects in a form board, that is, a board with holes shaped in geometric patterns. As the child moves up the scales, the extent of the motor responses is restricted, and more verbal and calculation responses are required. At the adult levels the emphasis on verbal responses is extremely great.

Scoring. The responses of the child are recorded verbatim or by use of symbols, if possible, by the examiner. To test a child efficiently it is necessary that the examiner score the responses of the child as the test continues. However, he still is required to spend about an additional hour in the process of scoring the entire instrument and writing his report, which may be quite lengthy.

The success of a child is expressed in terms of months of mental age. His mental age is, in reality, the chronological age at which the average child performs as well as the child in question. The test has been standardized in such a way as to establish this situation. The number of test items which the child successfully passes are scored in terms of the appropriate months of credit per test item, and his mental age is computed. His mental age is converted to an intelligence quotient (IQ) by referring to tables. The intelligence quotient of today is not a quotient at all, even though the name is retained. Originally, the IQ was the ratio between the child's mental age and chronological age multiplied by 100. Now the Stanford-Binet IQ is a standard score with an arithmetic mean of 100 and a standard deviation of 16. Insofar as the 1960 edition of the Stanford-Binet is concerned, approximately two-thirds of the IQ's in an unselected group would fall between a high of 116 and a low of 84; approximately ninety-nine per cent of the IQ's of this group would fall between a high of 148 and a low of 52.

Interpretation. The interpretation of the results of the administration of the Stanford-Binet Intelligence Scale is complex. Much more information is available than the intelligence quotient itself. The examiner writes a statement, sometimes of considerable length, describing the test performance of the subject. He is frequently able to indicate the types of items with which the child experiences considerable success and those with which he experiences less success. Also, he is able to offer an insight, however limited, into the personality characteristics of the child, for example, his tendencies to be easily frustrated, negativistic, warm and friendly, impulsive, inhibited. In comparison with the information produced by the typical group test of mental ability, the Stanford-Binet is a veritable gold mine. Frequently, the examiner can offer useful diagnostic interpretations which are of great help to the teacher and to the child's parents.

Validity of the Test. Surveys of the voluminous research concerning the three editions of the Stanford-Binet have yielded some interesting conclusions about its validity. Its predictive validity with regard to academic success is good. On the other hand, the picture of its construct validity is mixed. According to Cronbach,[4] the following statements can be made concerning the Stanford-Binet scale:

1. It measures present ability, not inborn capacity.
2. Its scores are strongly weighted with verbal abilities.
3. Its scores measure somewhat different mental abilities at different ages.
4. It requires experiences common to the U.S. urban culture and is of dubious value for comparing cultural groups.
5. It does not give a reliable measure of separate aspects of mentality.
6. Its scores are influenced by the child's personality and emotional habits.

The Wechsler scales. The Wechsler scales contain both verbal and performance subtests. Like the Stanford-Binet Intelligence Scale, these scales are individual tests and, when properly administered, offer considerable information about the subject.

There are two Wechsler scales of importance in education: the Wechsler Intelligence Scale for Children[5] and the Wechsler Adult Intelligence Scale.[6] In the case of the Wechsler Intelligence Scale for Children, the subtests are:

Verbal Tests	*Performance Tests*
General Information	Picture Completion
General Comprehension	Picture Arrangement
Arithmetic	Block Design
Similarities	Object Assembly
Vocabulary	Coding
Digit Span (Optional)	Mazes (Optional)

The Wechsler Adult Intelligence Scale contains the following subtests:

[4] Lee J. Cronbach, *Essentials of Psychological Testing,* 2nd ed. (New York: Harper & Brothers, Publishers, 1960), pp. 181–86.
[5] Published by The Psychological Corporation, New York, 1949.
[6] Published by The Psychological Corporation, New York, 1955.

Verbal Tests	*Performance Tests*
Information	Picture Arrangement
Comprehension	Picture Completion
Digit Span	Block Design
Similarities	Object Assembly
Arithmetic	Digit Symbol
Vocabulary	

Both Wechsler scales are more easily administered than the Stanford-Binet scale. However, they also require an extremely skilled and experienced examiner and involve a scoring problem in that judgments must be made as to the accuracy of responses, for example, in the case of the vocabulary test.

Like the Stanford-Binet Intelligence Scale, the Wechsler scales produce intelligence quotients. These are also standard score intelligence quotients. However, they have an arithmetic mean of 100 and a standard deviation of 15. Because the standard deviations differ, and because the tests have different standardization samples, the intelligence quotients from the Wechsler scales and those from the Stanford-Binet Intelligence Scale are not interchangeable. On the other hand, the Wechsler scales no doubt measure many of the same student characteristics as the Stanford-Binet scale. The verbal test IQ's correlate quite highly with the Stanford-Binet IQ's, whereas the correlation between these IQ's and the results of the performance tests is lower. This leads one to believe that the separate IQ's for the verbal and performance tests are measuring slightly different student characteristics. If small differences occur between the verbal and performance IQ's for an individual, they probably mean little. However, larger differences are interpretable. Bear in mind also that the subtests within the verbal scale and the performance scale are somewhat unreliable and, hence, interpretations of these profiles have very limited practical value unless the differences between subtest scores are extremely large.

As in the case of the Stanford-Binet Intelligence Scale, the Wechsler scales are customarily used when there is some unusual reason for wishing to measure the mental ability of the child in the most careful way. Time and expense prevent large groups of students from being administered tests of this sort. For the student with reasonable emotional stability and an adequate command of the English language the group tests of mental ability provide satisfactory information concerning this student characteristic.

Group Tests of Mental Ability

Hundreds of group tests of mental ability are available today. They cover the full range of formal education from kindergarten to graduate school. Some provide only a single score; others yield a profile of three or four subscores, each of which is thought to represent a different facet of mental ability. To understand fully the degree of construct validity which is possessed by each of these tests, one must examine them with considerable care. The following brief descriptions of selected tests of mental ability can serve as the first step in this recommended study of the test.

Elementary and secondary school tests. Most of the efforts to develop suitable mental ability tests are directed toward the elementary and secondary school needs. As a result, today there are mental ability tests which are relatively long and relatively short; which are almost entirely verbal or combine verbal aspects with nonverbal aspects; and which are exclusively designed for a small range of class levels or which provide a series of related forms to cover many class levels.

Readiness tests. Readiness tests can be thought of as aptitude tests constructed to serve a relatively restricted purpose. Rather than being designed to predict academic achievement in a wide variety of areas, they are intended to predict academic achievement in one or two restricted areas. For example, reading readiness tests are widely used in kindergarten and first grade of the elementary school. The Lee-Clark Reading Readiness Test[7] is thought to yield scores which assist the teacher in determining whether students entering the first grade are ready for reading instruction, or, if they are not, when formal reading instruction will be productive. The test involves visual discrimination and recognition of differences and similarities in letter symbols and word symbols.

The Metropolitan Readiness Tests[8] are more broadly oriented. The results from this test are thought to be useful for indicating those students who are likely to profit from formal instruction in

[7] Published by the California Test Bureau, Los Angeles, 1951.
[8] Published by Harcourt, Brace & World, Inc., New York, 1950.

reading and number work, as well as to identify those students who require additional instruction before they are ready for such work. The content of this test is entirely pictorial; approximately one hour is needed for its administration.

Single-score mental ability tests. Of the many single-score mental ability tests which are available, the Otis Quick-Scoring Mental Ability Tests[9] are among the most popular. Three levels are available: the Alpha Test for grades 1 to 4, the Beta Test for grades 5 to 9, and the Gamma Test for high school and college students.

In the case of each of the three tests, the test items are arranged according to the level of difficulty, irrespective of test item content. It is quite possible, therefore, for the student to encounter a vocabulary test item, following which is an arithmetic test item, and following that might be a verbal analogy test item. It is for this reason that the Otis tests are known as omnibus tests of intelligence. They sample a variety of mental traits without any particular attention to the similarity of test item content from test item to test item.

The Alpha Test (Short Form) is the only one of the three tests which is not self-administering. Also, it is the only one of the three tests which can be administered twice with two different sets of instructions so that verbal and nonverbal aspects of mental ability can be sampled. In the case of the nonverbal administration, the teacher instructs the students to examine the series of pictures contained in each test item and to draw a horizontal line through that picture in the series which is unlike the remaining pictures. A different set of instructions is read to the students for each test item for the verbal administration. The student responds by drawing a vertical line through the picture which represents his response to the test item. The verbal and nonverbal sections are scored and the two scores are added to obtain a total score. This can be expressed in terms of mental age, or an intelligence quotient can be derived.

Whereas the Alpha Test (Short Form) requires 25 minutes of working time, the Beta Test and the Gamma Test each require 30 minutes of time. The latter two are self-administering tests, that is, the test booklets are distributed and the students are allowed to study the first page with a minimum of direction, following which they

---

[9] Published by Harcourt, Brace & World, Inc., New York, 1953.

continue with the test. The content of the test is predominantly verbal in nature. Scoring the test yields mental age scores which can be converted into intelligence quotients. These have been shown to be of adequate reliability in spite of the fact that the working time for the tests is relatively short. Moreover, when the criterion is future academic achievement of a verbal nature, the degree of predictive validity of the test compares favorably with that of other group mental ability tests.

Double-score mental ability tests. Representing mental ability by means of a single score is obviously inadequate. Mental ability is certainly not a unitary entity. Recognition of this fact is becoming more and more evident in test construction today. The first step in this process was the splitting of the total score into two subscores, commonly verbal and nonverbal subscores or verbal and mathematical subscores. Certainly, these are important components of mental ability and have great potential with respect to predicting academic success.

One of the most popular double-score tests of mental ability is the California Test of Mental Maturity (CTMM).[10] Like most of its counterparts, it is a highly reliable measure of mental ability. It has a continuous series of levels, from kindergarten to adulthood. There are six such levels: Pre-primary (kindergarten, entering first grade), Primary (grades 1 to 3), Elementary (grades 4 to 8), Junior High (grades 7 to 9), Secondary (grades 9 to 13), and Advanced (grades 10 to adulthood).

The test contains twelve subtests which are classified in five areas: memory, spatial relationships, logical reasoning, numerical reasoning, and verbal concepts. The results of the tests can be reported in terms of mental ages and intelligence quotients for language and nonlanguage components as well as for the total test. The subscores for the five areas are sometimes claimed to be a suitable profile of these student abilities; however, evidence in support of this claim is not available. Consequently, these subscores are virtually ignored.

Although the California Test of Mental Maturity includes a wide variety of test items and is well standardized, the language and nonlanguage intelligence quotients are very similar. Because

[10] Published by the California Test Bureau, Los Angeles, 1957.

of this, they are not as effective in educational diagnosis as one would hope. Their ineffectiveness prevents the drawing of far-reaching conclusions concerning the relationship between a language IQ and academic achievement heavily involving language, and between a nonlanguage IQ and academic achievement not heavily related to language skills. Generally speaking, therefore, the most important score from the California Test of Mental Maturity is the total IQ.

Instead of speaking of language and nonlanguage components of mental ability, the School and College Ability Tests (SCAT)[11] are oriented in a slightly different direction. The purpose of these tests is to provide information concerning the student's capacity to perform academic tasks in the future. Hence, the test is designed directly in terms of verbal and quantitative components of mental ability. The verbal section samples the student's vocabulary and his reading comprehension, whereas the quantitative section samples his arithmetic reasoning power and his ability to solve computational problems. The test actually contains four parts, two devoted to the verbal section and two devoted to the quantitative section.

The School and College Ability Tests are available in five levels ranging from the fourth grade to college sophomores. The five levels correspond exactly to those used in the achievement test battery known as the Sequential Tests of Educational Progress (STEP). Since these mental ability tests are standardized on the basis of the same students used to standardize the achievement tests, we have available an unusually effective team of tests. Interpreting student achievement in terms of student mental ability is greatly strengthened when all tests are based on the same standardization group. Ordinarily, this is not the case. The SCAT-STEP team is a welcomed exception.

The results of the School and College Ability Tests are not reported as intelligence quotients but as converted scores and percentiles. The most effective way of analyzing the results is by means of the band technique described in Chapter III. Both achievement scores and the two general ability scores can be quickly examined in terms of overlapping bands and probability interpretations can be made.

---

[11] Published by the Cooperative Test Division of the Educational Testing Service, Princeton, New Jersey, 1955.

The School and College Ability Tests have, for the most part, a greater educational loading than does the California Test of Mental Maturity. The School and College Ability Tests are good illustrations of the mental ability testing philosophy that the best way to determine a student's potential in formal education is to examine related aspects of his achievement today.

Factor-analytic mental ability tests. What is the composition of mental ability? Certainly, the answer to this question cannot be given today. On the other hand, important steps have been taken which are steadily clarifying the nature of the concept known as mental ability. Years ago Spearman devoted his research to the isolation of the basic component of mental ability which he called general ability or "g." With his work began the use of statistical techniques known as factor analysis. Later, Thurstone perfected a factor analytic approach and used it to develop tests to measure a student's "primary mental abilities." Thurstone wanted to discover those relatively unrelated components of mental ability and to design a suitable subtest for each. As a result of many studies, he identified seven such factors:

1. Verbal-meaning (Ability to understand ideas expressed in words).
2. Perception (Ability to recognize likenesses and differences between objects and symbols with ease and without hesitation).
3. Quantitative (Ability to understand the meaning of numbers and to recognize quantitative differences).
4. Number (Ability to work with numbers and to handle simple quantitative problems rapidly and accurately).
5. Motor (Ability to coordinate hand and eye movements).
6. Space (Ability to visualize and to think about objects in two or three dimensions).
7. Reasoning (Ability to solve logical problems).

There are now three levels of the primary mental abilities tests available for general use.[12] The first level is for children of ages five to seven and provides scores for five of the seven abilities listed in the foregoing paragraph. These are verbal-meaning, space perception, motor, and quantitative. The second level, designed for ages seven to eleven, provides measures in the following five areas: verbal-meaning, space, reasoning, perception, and number. The

[12] Published by the Science Research Associates, Chicago, 1946–1958.

most recently published of the three levels is that designed for ages eleven to seventeen. This level is intended to measure verbal-meaning, space, reasoning, number, and word-fluency. The results of all three levels of the test are expressed in terms of a general ability quotient, which is thought to be comparable to the intelligence quotient.

Ideally, the profile provided by the five subscores would offer diagnostic possibilities as well as a more efficient basis upon which to predict academic achievement in specific areas. In reality, this high level of utility is not realized. The primary abilities as isolated by Thurstone are not completely unrelated to each other. Seemingly, each is a composite of an independent primary ability and a general factor similar, if not identical, to that investigated by Spearman. This causes the correlations between the various factors to be higher than desirable and, hence, reduces the diagnostic possibilities.

The predictive validity of the primary mental ability tests does not exceed that found with mental ability tests providing one or two scores. However, there is considerable potential here. Indeed, it is safe to say that the modern trend in mental ability testing is in the direction of developing more and better factor-analytic tests which will offer reasonably complete profiles of student mental ability and which will allow teachers, counselors, and parents to predict academic achievement in a differential manner.

The ultimate outcome of efforts to develop better factor-analytic tests is, of course, difficult to predict. Interesting speculation with regard to this, however, can be made on the basis of Guilford's organization of intellectual tasks.[13] He visualizes five types of mental operation, with the tasks related to each type classified as "content" and "product." The types of mental operation are: (1) Memory; (2) Cognition; (3) Convergent thinking; (4) Divergent thinking; and (5) Evaluation.

For "content" categories he lists figural, symbolic, semantic, and behavioral; his "products" are units of information, classes of units, relations between units, systems of information, transformations, and implications. Guilford's classification involves 120 different combinations, each of which represents a test construction pos-

[13] J. P. Guilford, "A Revised Structure of Intellect," Reports from the Psychological Laboratory of the University of Southern California, No. 19 (1957).

sibility. If Guilford's classification or one similar to it is widely adopted, then a short list of primary abilities is probably a gross misrepresentation of the true complexity of mental ability.

Mental ability tests in higher education. Although the use of standardized achievement tests in higher education is relatively small, the same is not true of mental ability tests. The question of selecting the most suitable freshman class and the question of admitting only those applicants for graduate school who are likely to succeed, have caused greater and greater emphasis to be placed on the role of mental abilities in higher education. This has been particularly true in recent years. More and more colleges and universities are adopting selective admissions policies, and more and more graduate schools are finding their facilities badly taxed by increasing enrollments and, consequently, are tightening admission requirements. Many sources are being tapped for evidence concerning the talent and motivation of the prospective undergraduate or graduate student. Primary among these are the data produced by mental ability tests, for example, in the case of the undergraduate, the Scholastic Aptitude Tests (SAT) of the College Entrance Examination Board,[14] the College Qualification Tests,[15] and the American College Testing Program.[16]

The College Entrance Examination Board Admissions Testing Program is the best known of the college admissions programs. Today almost 300 colleges and universities require scores from this program as a part of the total information provided by the student when he requests admission to that institution. These colleges and universities are primarily located in the eastern section of the United States and enroll about twenty per cent of all undergraduate students.

The core of the total program is the Scholastic Aptitude Test which yields two scores, one in the verbal area and one in the mathematical area. Also included in the program are thirteen achievement tests, of which the student may select as many as three or as few as none. These tests cover the areas of biology, chemistry, English composition, French, German, Greek, Italian, Latin, inter-

[14] Administered by the Educational Testing Service, Princeton, New Jersey.
[15] Published by The Psychological Corporation, New York, 1956.
[16] Developed by E. F. Lindquist and T. McCarrel of the State University of Iowa, Iowa City, Iowa.

mediate mathematics, advanced mathematics, physics, social studies, and Spanish.

The tests included in this testing program are restricted and not available for general examination. The Scholastic Aptitude Test is administered six times annually, whereas the achievement tests are administered four times annually.

The verbal section of the Scholastic Aptitude Test measures the student's vocabulary and verbal reasoning power, whereas the mathematical section measures his knowledge of high school mathematics and his quantitative reasoning power. The degree of predictive validity of these scores is adequate but not outstanding. This is no doubt due to the fact that the students for whom achievement test scores are available are quite highly selected and, therefore, the size of the coefficients of predictive validity tends to be depressed.

Although the College Entrance Examination Board Admissions Testing Program has been in operation a number of years, it is used primarily in the eastern half of the country. A relatively new testing program known as the American College Testing Program is gaining acceptance in the western half of the nation for the most part. The test battery used in this program differs from that used in the College Entrance Examination Board program in that fewer tests are included. The American College Testing Program contains only four tests, each with a heavy educational loading. The subtests are directed toward the areas of English, mathematics, social studies, and natural sciences; and the profile of scores is considered to be useful in college admission decisions, scholarship awards, and in placement of the students in freshman classes.

Differential Aptitude Test Batteries

In addition to mental ability, teachers, parents, and counselors are, on occasion, quite interested in other student aptitudes, for example, mechanical and clerical aptitudes. Group tests are available in areas such as these and can be administered when desired. On the other hand, if there is a widespread feeling that information with respect to such aptitudes is important, then a battery of aptitude tests is administered. This battery includes some of the components of mental ability already discussed, as well as some of the aptitude areas sometimes thought to be of secondary importance in formal education.

There are three outstanding differential aptitude test batteries which have provided useful information in the secondary school. These are the Differential Aptitude Tests (DAT),[17] the General Aptitude Test Battery (GATB),[18] and the Flanagan Aptitude Classification Tests (FACT).[19] The first of the three is easily the most popular of the group so far as secondary school test administration is concerned.

The Differential Aptitude Tests are eight in number:

Verbal Reasoning	Mechanical Reasoning
Numerical Ability	Clerical Speed and Accuracy
Abstract Reasoning	Language Usage (Spelling)
Space Relations	Language Usage (Sentences)

Note that the last is divided into two subtests, namely, spelling and sentences. It is the purpose of the Differential Aptitude Tests to provide a profile of the relative strengths and weaknesses of a student in order that adequate predictions can be made of his future academic success and that, insofar as it is possible, the student may be assisted in making proper vocational choices.

The Differential Aptitude Tests are not factor-analytic tests. They are, however, very highly developed tests which are, in a number of instances, related to each other to only a moderate degree. This means that the interpretation of the profile of the eight scores is meaningful. Moreover, the wide variety of complex abilities which are measured by the various subtests have, on the surface at least, a useful relationship with an equally wide variety of educational and vocational tasks. As a result, the Differential Aptitude Tests are found to be quite versatile.

The predictive validity of the scores yielded by the Differential Aptitude Tests is reasonably good. Although no total score is available, many teachers and counselors combine the verbal reasoning score and the numerical ability score and use this composite for

[17] Published by The Psychological Corporation, New York, 1947.
[18] Published and Administered by the United States Employment Service.
[19] Published by the Science Research Associates, Chicago, 1953.

the purpose of predicting future academic success. Notice that this policy is consistent with that sometimes followed in other group mental ability tests.

The General Aptitude Test Battery is quite different from the Differential Aptitude Tests. This battery reflects some of the findings of the Thurstone factor-analytic investigations. Although it is administered by the United States Employment Service primarily for its occupational counseling program, a cooperative plan with secondary schools is sometimes established by means of which the battery is administered to juniors and seniors in high school. It should be remembered, of course, that the battery is fundamentally oriented toward the problem of assisting a person to find a suitable vocation. Because of the variability of talents required by the many vocations under consideration, a battery of tests of considerable scope is needed.

The current edition of the General Aptitude Test Battery contains eight paper-and-pencil tests and four apparatus tests. Nine factors are thought to be measured:

G—General Reasoning Ability
V—Verbal Aptitude
N—Numerical Aptitude
S—Spatial Aptitude
P—Form Perception
Q—Clerical Perception
K—Motor Coordination
F—Finger Dexterity
M—Manual Dexterity

The eight paper-and-pencil tests are:

Vocabulary (Knowledge of English vocabulary).

Arithmetic Reasoning (Solution of verbal problems involving number relationships).

Computation (Solution of number problems).

Three-Dimensional Space (Visual manipulation of objects in space).

Name Comparison (Detection of discrepancies between two lists of names).

Tool Matching (Visual comparison of pictures of tools).

Form Matching (Matching identical forms).

Mark Making (Making vertical marks in squares).

The four apparatus tests are:

Place (Transferring pegs from one pegboard to another).
Turn (Inverting pegs while transferring to second pegboard).
Assemble (Fitting rivets and washers in holes).
Disassemble (Replacing rivets in a bin and washers on a rod).

The General Aptitude Test Battery is an extremely efficient battery in that it requires less than two and one-half hours for the administration of all tests. The amount of time allowed for the paper-and-pencil tests is about six minutes for each. The relationships between the various subtests are relatively low; consequently, as in the case of the Differential Aptitude Tests, meaningful interpretations of the resulting profiles can be made. These interpretations very often are of immeasurable help when the classroom teacher attempts to evaluate student achievement in terms of student potential and when the school counselor attempts to assist the student in the process of making educational and vocational decisions.

CHAPTER VI

School-Wide Testing Programs

If a teacher truly believes that evaluation is an integral part of the teaching art, and if he tries to orient his activities accordingly, he soon discovers that some degree of order and system is needed so that his evaluation efforts will be effective to the maximum degree. In many respects, each individual teacher can introduce his own system and, therefore, attempt to arrive at maximum efficiency in his own way. On the other hand, since he shares students with other teachers, he must coordinate his evaluation efforts with these teachers. This coordination generally occurs in the realm of final marks and in the realm of standardized achievement and aptitude tests. The latter is of primary interest since it is the heart of school-wide testing programs.

In its simplest form, the school-wide testing program is a small number of standardized achievement and aptitude tests which are administered in a wholesale fashion to the students of a given school at more or less regular intervals. Some programs are so limited that only group tests of mental ability are administered once, or perhaps twice, in the course of a twelve-year public school program. Others are so elaborate that "testing weeks" are set aside at the beginning of the school year and at the end of the school year for the administration of a complete battery of achievement, aptitude, and personal-social adjustment instruments. The total cost of such a program for even a moderate-sized school district can be thousands of dollars.

Currently, there is a movement to enlarge and strengthen the school-wide testing programs. The impetus for this movement can be traced to a large extent to the National Defense Education Act of 1958. It is quite probable that this is just the beginning of a long-range movement to raise the school-wide testing programs of the public schools to a level which will allow them to operate efficiently in a technological age.

Although the public schools are experiencing considerable growth with regard to testing programs, the same is not true of these programs in higher education. In only a few colleges and universities is there any systematic effort to test student achievement and aptitude beyond those efforts which are included in the freshman testing program administered in September of the freshman year. Those institutions which have an expanded testing program are oftentimes a part of the Institutional Testing Program of the Graduate Record Examinations.[1] This program includes the aptitude test, the advanced achievement tests, and a series of three area tests. The area tests cover three fields: social science, humanities, and natural science.

In a number of colleges and universities the scope of the freshman testing program is actually contracting. Because of selective admissions policies, more and more of these institutions are requiring the students to submit aptitude and, possibly, achievement test scores with their application, which is processed in the spring preceding the fall entrance date. Special tests for placement purposes and, sometimes, tests in the area of personal-social adjustment are administered during freshman week to supplement the information already available with the admission form.

The following discussion of school-wide testing programs is restricted to the public school scene. The purpose and nature of such programs often vary slightly from one school system to another. Generally speaking, however, these variations are minor.

Purposes of the Testing Program

As one would logically expect, the purposes of the school-wide testing program are tied directly and completely to the educational objectives of the public school system. In the last analysis the results of the testing program are to be used as a partial basis for evaluating the degree to which the students achieve the objectives which guide the instructional program in which they participate. This evaluation becomes more and more meaningful as educators are able to utilize more and more background information concerning the student. Certainly, the degree to which a student achieves should be evaluated in the light of his aptitude, interests, and motivation. The environmental situation which he experiences should also be in-

[1] Administered by the Educational Testing Service, Princeton, New Jersey.

cluded. Although such information is not acquired as a part of the school-wide testing program, it is commonly recorded on the same form and placed in the same folder as the test scores produced by the school-wide testing program.

Since testing programs are, with rare exceptions, composed exclusively of paper-and-pencil tests, it follows that the test results are applicable to the evaluation of student achievement with respect to verbal and mathematical objectives only. Indeed, some of these are not involved since appropriate tests are not included in the testing program. Therefore, even some of the most elaborate testing programs provide information concerning student behavior with respect to a relatively limited number of educational goals.

To utilize fully the information yielded by a testing program, the school system in question must design the program with great care by first examining the scope and importance of the school system's educational objectives of a verbal and mathematical nature. From these objectives are selected those for which suitable standardized achievement tests are available. This means that the core of the testing program is a battery of achievement tests in the basic skill areas. Although paper-and-pencil tests in the personal-social adjustment area are notably weak, they are sometimes included for the purpose of providing information concerning student behavior with respect to certain pertinent educational objectives or, if not for this reason, for the purpose of providing background information concerning the student in order to strengthen the evaluation of his educational achievement.

Standardized aptitude tests are obviously not included for the purpose of measuring the student's academic success. Instead, they are included for the primary purpose of providing a more complete interpretation of the achievement test scores and, hence, a more complete evaluation of the student's academic success.

Nature of the Testing Program

Much has been written concerning the scope of the testing program, the selection of the tests to be included, the administration and scoring of the tests, and the recording of the test results.[2] It is

[2] Arthur E. Traxler, *et al., Introduction to Testing and the Use of Test Results in Public Schools* (New York: Harper & Brothers, Publishers, 1953); and Arthur E. Traxler, "Ten Essential Steps in a Testing Program," *Education,* 79

already clear that the achievement and aptitude testing areas heavily dominate school testing programs. Sometimes interest inventories and, on rare occasions, personality inventories are added to this hard core.

The decision to include achievement and aptitude tests in the school testing program gives rise to a series of practical questions concerning the selection of the tests, their administration and scoring, and the recording of the test results. For instance, of the many tests available, which should be purchased and administered? What administrative machinery is needed to facilitate the administration, scoring, and recording tasks? To what degree are these duties a part of the professional activities of the classroom teacher, counselor, and the school administrator? Should the test scores be released to students and parents? Questions such as these are, of course, not answered in the same fashion by every school system, yet experience has demonstrated that there are certain useful principles which can serve as guides when establishing a testing program.

Selection of tests. A number of attempts have been made to organize and simplify the steps to be followed when selecting a standardized achievement or aptitude test from among a relatively large group of them.[3] From the hundreds of tests which are available, only one or two are to be chosen. How can the proper selection be made?

The first step to be followed which greatly improves the likelihood of making the proper selection is to specify that the decision will be a group decision rather than an individual decision. No matter how insightful a principal or a counselor may be, he should not be allowed to assume the responsibility of selecting the tests to be included in the school testing program. It is quite logical that all of the educational personnel who are involved in the testing program should also be involved in the selection of the test. This means that the school administration staff, the counselor staff, and each of the

(February 1959), pp. 357–61; and Educational Testing Service, *Essential Characteristics of a Program,* Evaluation and Advisory Service Series, No. 2 (Princeton, N.J.: Educational Testing Service, 1956).

[3] Educational Testing Service, *Selecting an Achievement Test: Principles and Procedures,* Evaluation and Advisory Service Series, No. 3 (Princeton, N.J.: Educational Testing Service, 1958).

major subject-matter departments should be represented on a committee charged with the task of finding those tests which will satisfy the purposes of the testing program to the greatest degree.

This committee has available huge quantities of information, both from advertising sources as well as from the professional literature. In the case of the latter category, the *Mental Measurements Yearbooks,* the psychological and educational journals, and a large body of books devoted to tests and measurements can be consulted. From this broad screening process comes a relatively small handful of prime candidates for the testing program. These tests must be scrutinized with great care. A helpful approach is to tabulate in a systematic fashion a large group of pertinent information concerning the test. Some committees use printed forms for this purpose, whereas others will be less formal in the organization of this information.

The information needed about each test falls into six broad categories in practically all cases. These are (1) information of a general nature, (2) information concerning the design of the test, (3) information concerning the validity of the test, (4) information concerning the reliability of the test, (5) information concerning the test norms, and (6) miscellaneous information such as reviewers' comments and bibliographical references.

The general information category includes the title of the test, the names of its author and publisher, and the titles of the forms and levels. Also recorded are the cost, the time required, and the nature of the scoring. To describe the design of the test, it is necessary to describe the purpose of the test, the basis for selecting the test items, the type of test item, and the manner of administration.

In order to summarize information concerning the validity of the test, one must first carefully identify the purpose for which the test scores are to be used and then examine available information concerning all pertinent validity determinations with respect to the test in question. Certainly, a number of the validity determinations reported may not be meaningful with regard to the test selection problem, since the purpose for which the use of the scores is intended is not the same as the purpose of the testing program. Also, when evaluating a validity determination which seems to be meaningful in terms of the purposes identified, the important characteristics of the examinees involved in the validity determination must be reported. It is clear that these examinees must be in all major respects very similar to the students to be involved in the school testing program in order for the validity determination to be meaningful.

The categories of information concerning reliability norms are somewhat similar to the validity category. Again, the purposes for which the testing program is being organized guide any determination of the adequacy of the reliability or the suitability of the tables of norms reported.

Finally, the category of miscellaneous information may offer little in a routine investigation of tests, but it may provide highly suitable leads if a depth study is being made of a given instrument with regard to some of its pertinent characteristics. Bibliographical references which otherwise may only be reported as a matter of form suddenly become sources of a wide variety of interesting information.

After all available information concerning the outstanding tests has been tabulated, it may be immediately apparent as to which test should be finally chosen. On the other hand, an important amount of doubt may still remain. In either event, an item-by-item study of the tests should be conducted. Under no circumstances should so important a decision be made without exhausting every possible source of information. Just as no one would purchase an automobile without test-driving it, no one should purchase a test without administering it to himself. Although it is not possible to play the role of the student in a completely meaningful manner, the teacher can still approach this position to a sufficient degree to be rewarded by a far deeper insight into the test under consideration when he himself attempts to write the answers to its test items.

Administration of the tests. The same committee which selected the tests may wish to govern the administrative practices to be followed when the testing program is conducted. It is a wise procedure, however, to appoint a director of the program to handle the myriad of administrative details necessarily incurred when a testing program is being administered. His duties are to translate the policies of the advisory committee into actual practice. Also, it is his responsibility that the tests are properly administered. If teachers administer the tests, he must train them most carefully in regard to test etiquette and discipline. Teachers are commonly too lax when timing the test and too cooperative when answering student questions.

The time of year at which the testing program is to be administered is debated by teachers, counselors, and students alike. The general consensus is that fall testing is preferred in all cases except those in which course-orientated standardized achievement tests are being administered. Thus, scholastic aptitude tests and achievement tests measuring basic skills or broad achievement areas should be administered in the fall, whereas achievement tests in specific subject-matter areas, such as American history and geometry, should be administered in the spring.

The frequency with which the aptitude and achievement tests are administered is also a subject of much discussion among educational personnel. There is considerable sentiment for a yearly testing program involving both standardized achievement and mental ability tests. Because of a number of practical testing problems, such a program would not start in kindergarten, but in the third or fourth grade. Another point of view with regard to the frequency of the administration of the testing program is that, starting in the third grade, achievement tests should be administered annually, whereas the mental ability tests should be administered in grades 3, 6, 9, and 11. Both points of view agree that in the second semester of the kindergarten or the first semester of first grade, a readiness test should be administered to all students.

The first of the two foregoing plans is criticized on the basis that it represents an overemphasis upon standardized achievement and aptitude testing. Considerable resentment exists in some school districts on this score, particularly if, in addition to the school-wide testing program, the students are also engaged in a city-wide or state-wide testing program composed of different tests. In instances such as these, students have been known to spend a week or more in the process of writing a series of tests, many of which clearly overlap each other.

Widespread complaint exists with regard to the concentration of testing present in many high schools in the second half of the eleventh grade and the first half of the twelfth grade. College-bound students interested in scholarships sometimes write so many tests that they become badly preoccupied in this respect and, as a result, their normal academic achievement during this time suffers. In all probability, this situation will be relieved at least moderately as organized testing programs such as that sponsored by the College Entrance Examination Board and the American College Testing Program receive wider acceptance.

Scoring and recording the results. Scoring objective tests is a strictly clerical job. If at all possible, the classroom teacher should not be involved in this task. A skilled clerk will very likely score the student responses more accurately and more rapidly than teachers who, after all, are employed to perform far more creative activities.

Because of the rapid growth of standardized testing in the recent past and the likely continued growth in the foreseeable future, test scoring agencies have been organized on a large scale and are capable of providing excellent service. In some states there is a central office with scoring machines such as the IBM 9902 Test Scoring Machine. Such offices are willing and capable of handling test scoring problems in a relatively efficient manner.

In other instances school districts have utilized the services of a test scoring organization such as the Measurement Research Center, Inc.[4] This is a nonprofit corporation which is capable of scoring the answer sheets from local, state-wide, and national testing programs. This is accomplished with an amazing degree of efficiency by means of electronic test scoring machines and related equipment. In addition to the lists of students' scores, test scoring centers such as this are capable of preparing and reporting local norms, computing and reporting average scores for each school in the school system or for the entire system, and preparing punched IBM cards for each student.

Clearly, test scoring is now a highly refined technique. It is only because of this that state and national testing programs of considerable scope are capable of being conducted. The speed and accuracy of the process are unparalleled. Generally speaking, the most time-consuming element in the entire operation is the time required by the United States Post Office to transport the answer sheets to the test scoring center and then back to the school system. The accuracy improvements over teacher scoring efforts occurred not only in the

[4] Organized by E. F. Lindquist, State University of Iowa, Iowa City, Iowa.

computation of the students' raw score, but also in the transcribing and reporting of the test results.

Recording the test results is also a clerical task. Machine methods have not been particularly helpful here. Since it is necessary that the test scores be recorded along with the other educational and environmental information needed to interpret them, an elaborate record keeping system must be inaugurated and continually maintained. The common means of accomplishing this task is the cumulative record.[5] This record takes many forms and varies in the nature and amount of information it is designed to contain. Generally speaking, however, it has sections devoted to personal information concerning the student, his health record, his family background, his final marks and deportment record, and the results of the standardized achievement and aptitude tests which have been administered to him periodically in his educational program. The sections devoted to recording the standardized test results provide space for noting the date, the class level, the name of the test, the level of the test, the form of the test, and all of the subtest scores and total scores, along with the identification of the norm groups which were used.

Ideally, the cumulative records are so stored and so controlled that teachers, counselors, and administrators can readily obtain them and use them in student and parent conferences. Only if this is true can the full potential of the school testing program be realized. Regrettably, some school officials treat test scores as highly classified information. They assume that the scores should be protected at all costs, thereby automatically preventing the major purposes of the testing program from being realized.

No one will deny that there is good reason to restrict the distribution and use of standardized test results to those people who have a legitimate reason for needing to know their sizes and patterns. Debate arises when the question is asked with respect to which individuals have such legitimate reasons. There is much evidence to favor including the parents in this group, provided that the nature of the test, the purposes for administering the test, and the mean-

[5] Mildred L. Fisher, "The Cumulative Record as a Tool," in *The Yearbook of the Association of Supervisors of Curriculum Development* (1955), pp. 147–73; and State Committee on Cumulative Records, *Handbook on California Cumulative Records* (Sacramento: California State Department of Education, 1956).

ing of the norms have been carefully and thoroughly explained to them.[6]

Uses of Test Results

The uses of test results can be divided into two groups: classroom uses and administrative uses. The first group is the more important by a wide margin since it reflects the primary purpose of the existence of school testing programs, namely, to assist in the evaluation of student achievement with respect to verbal and mathematical educational goals of considerable importance. The outstanding administrative uses are (1) general evaluations of the over-all educational program insofar as its verbal and mathematical components are concerned and (2) general interpretations of the school to the community by means of objective data concerning academic achievement.

Classroom uses of test scores. Classroom teachers use standardized achievement test scores in many different ways, some of which are outstandingly successful and some of which have little to recommend them. Using test results, such as mental ability scores and reading speed and comprehension scores, for the purpose of sectioning students enrolled in courses requiring a considerable amount of verbal facility is a practice which has received wide acceptance. On the other hand, using standardized achievement tests as end-of-course examinations or as the sole basis for determining final marks is a highly dangerous practice and undoubtedly leads to serious misrepresentations of student academic success.

Another successful classroom use of test scores is the evaluation of academic success in terms of mental ability. Many teachers find that their grasp of the degree of a given student's academic success is greatly increased, because they are able to compare the level of his mental ability with the level of his academic success. Wide discrepancies between potential and achievement offer the first step in an interesting and profitable study of that student's career in that school system. Quite likely, such an investigation would reveal the need for special remedial instruction in the case of the student whose potential far exceeds his achievement. Studies of those students whose achievement far outstrips their potential can provide

---

[6] James H. Ricks, Jr., "On Telling Parents About Test Results," *Test Service Bulletin,* No. 54 (December 1959), pp. 1–4.

interesting insight into the complexity of the teacher-pupil relationship.

Administrative uses of test scores. The chief school officer is responsible for the adequacy of the instructional program in his school system. In view of the diverse nature of the informal achievement test, he must turn to standardized achievement tests as a basis for determining the quality of his instructional program. Averaging the achievement test scores from class to class and school to school and comparing them with average mental ability scores offers a limited, but useful, view of the relative success of the students and of the instructional program. This information can also be of unusual value to school boards and parent-teacher organizations. At least, in terms of the verbal and mathematical aspects of the school program, they are obtaining factual evidence of the end products which their tax dollars are buying.

It is easy to understand the vital role that can be played by standardized achievement and aptitude test scores in the public relations program of the school system. If such scores are reported inaccurately or incompletely, much more confusion than enlightenment will result, and invidious comparisons between and among teachers and schools usually occur. On the other hand, if the summary of the achievement and aptitude test scores is prepared and interpreted with extreme care, a firm foundation is prepared for an intelligent analysis of the verbal and mathematical aspects of the school program and, hence, for the formulation of long-range planning to improve those aspects of the instructional program which seem less satisfactory.

The use of standardized achievement test scores for the purpose of evaluating teacher effectiveness is a stormy issue. If this evaluation is done indiscriminately, great injustices can result, in spite of the fact that a school-wide testing program seems extremely comprehensive. When the total goals of a teaching program are codified, it is clear that the standardized testing program is related to only a part of them, although an important part. Should the total effectiveness of a teacher be evaluated on this basis, it is likely that an unfair conclusion may be drawn.

One definition of effective teaching is that the effective teacher is that teacher whose students move to the greatest degree in the direction of desirable goals. Since paper-and-pencil achievement tests reflect the degree to which students have moved toward desirable verbal and mathematical goals, the tests thus become the beginning of a means to identify effective teaching. However, until a large family of effective evaluation instruments is developed which yield evidence with regard to all of the other educational goals, evaluation of teacher effectiveness in terms of this definition is very incomplete.

Diagnosis Based on Test Results

The diagnosis of student deficiencies in academic achievement is one of the teacher's most difficult tasks, and it is probably for this reason that some writers have devoted considerable attention to the problem.[7] In order to attack this task intelligently the teacher needs a wealth of information. This includes all that is available in the cumulative record of the student, as well as that from miscellaneous sources such as anecdotal records, work samples, correspondence, and conference reports. Beyond doubt, one of the most important segments of this body of information is that yielded by standardized achievement and aptitude tests. Even this information is surprisingly inadequate if it is not supplemented by considerable information concerning the student's personal-social adjustment.

From the point of view of diagnosis, the total score on an achievement test is only of slight assistance. If subtest scores are available, and if they reflect reasonably homogeneous segments of subject matter and student skills, then the diagnostic value of the information is greatly improved. In the last analysis, however, the achievement test results have a high utility in diagnosis only when the test is originally designed for diagnostic purposes, as, for example, the Diagnostic Tests and Self-Helps in Arithmetic.[8] In this case, there are actually twenty-three diagnostic tests which cover addition, subtraction, multiplication, and division of whole numbers, fractions, and decimals. On the basis of the information yielded by this test, the elementary school teacher has objective information obtained

---

[7] Glenn M. Blair, *Diagnostic and Remedial Teaching* (New York: The Macmillan Company, 1956); and Leo J. Brueckner and Guy L. Bond, *The Diagnosis and Treatment of Learning Difficulties* (New York: Appleton-Century-Crofts, Inc., 1955).

[8] Published by the California Test Bureau, Los Angeles, 1955.

in an efficient manner concerning the strength and weaknesses of the arithmetic achievement of the student.

Diagnosis usually begins on the basis of the entire class to whom the test was administered. Profiles of class achievement are constructed, which is usually followed by tabulating the response to each item by each student in the class. Test items which have been answered correctly by the vast majority of the group and those which have been answered incorrectly by the vast majority of the group are identified, and inferences are drawn concerning the causes of this situation. Close inspection of the wrong responses made in the case of those items which are frequently answered incorrectly provides additional insight into the reasons for the undesirable achievement. Such an analysis as this can be easily obtained when the results of the school-wide testing program are scored by machine methods.

Following the examination of class achievement as a whole, the teacher can repeat the process for each individual student. Because of the pressure of his duties, the teacher is generally able to scrutinize the achievement pattern of only a minority of his students. In the case of each of these, he systematically tallies the right and wrong responses made by the student and cross references them with the type of subject matter and behavioral change involved. Frequently, analyses of this kind reveal that the errors are concentrated in certain parts of the subject matter and, sometimes, in one type of behavioral change.

No statistical analysis of this type of data is recommended, nor is it needed. Instead, the information provides the basis for detailed general impressions on the part of the teacher with respect to the student's academic achievement, and it allows that teacher to engage in a series of profitable conferences with the student and with the student's parents. These conferences, in all probability, are the first step in the remedial teaching program. Once the teacher has had a chance to interpret the profile of the student's achievement in terms of his abilities, his personal-social adjustment, and pertinent environmental factors, he is then able to plan with the student an appropriate remedial program in order to correct his scholastic deficiencies.

Over-achievers and under-achievers. Student achievement should be interpreted in terms of student mental ability whenever possible.

If there are noticeable discrepancies between level of achievement and level of mental ability, there is automatically a very good reason for additional careful scrutiny of the academic career of the student. Students whose achievement level noticeably surpasses their mental ability level are known as over-achievers. For those for whom the level of achievement and mental ability are approximately the same, the title of normal-achievers is used. When the level of achievement is noticeably lower than the level of mental ability, the student is identified as an under-achiever.

The psychological and educational literature is replete with studies concerning over- and under-achievers. The means of identifying operationally the over- and under-achiever vary, but in many cases a statistical technique known as linear regression is applied. Moreover, the majority of the studies classify the students in terms of their over-all academic achievement. No effort is made to determine whether a given student is an over-achiever in one subject-matter area, perhaps a normal-achiever in another, and an under-achiever in still a third.

In recent years more efforts have been made to specify more carefully the nature of the over- and under-achievement.[9] Well-developed techniques are now available for predicting academic success in each of a number of subject-matter areas on the basis of a group of aptitude tests. In other words, if the degree of differential predictive validity is adequate, differential over- and under-achievement can be identified. This is a far more helpful approach in the analysis of student achievement than is the traditional method of determining over- and under-achievement in terms of over-all academic achievement.

The use of the results of standardized achievement and aptitude tests in the diagnosis of student achievement re-emphasizes the principle that the educational application of psychological tests is inevitably student oriented. Educational goals, both general and specific, are designed in terms of the necessity of helping a student learn how to satisfy his many needs. The informal and standardized

---

[9] William C. Krathwohl, "Specificity of Over- and Under-Achievement in College Courses," *Journal of Applied Psychology*, 36 (April 1952), pp. 103–6; and Paul Horst, "A Technique for the Development of a Differential Prediction Battery," *Psychological Monographs*, 68 (1954); and Paul Horst, "The Differential Prediction of Success in Various College Course Areas," *College and University*, 31 (1956), pp. 456–71.

tests administered to the student provide information concerning the degree to which he is moving toward these desired goals. Diagnosis of his position is conducted in the hope that the information contributed by standardized tests and other evaluation instruments will materially improve the grasp which teachers, counselors, administrators, and parents have of the student's scholastic progress and will serve as a basis for designing an efficient and mutually profitable remedial instructional program.

Bibliography

GENERAL REFERENCES

Ahmann, J. Stanley, and Marvin D. Glock, *Evaluating Pupil Growth.* Boston: Allyn & Bacon, Inc., 1959.

Ahmann, J. Stanley, Marvin D. Glock, and Helen L. Wardeberg, *Evaluating Elementary School Pupils.* Boston: Allyn & Bacon, Inc., 1960.

Anastasi, Anne, *Psychological Testing,* 2nd ed. New York: The Macmillan Company, 1961.

Cronbach, L. J., *Essentials of Psychological Testing,* 2nd ed. New York: Harper & Brothers, 1960.

Gardner, Eric F., *et al.,* "Educational and Psychological Testing," *Review of Educational Research,* 32 (February 1962), pp. 1–114.

Wrightstone, J. Wayne, *et al.,* "Educational Measurements," *Review of Educational Research,* 26 (June 1956), pp. 268–91.

EDUCATIONAL OBJECTIVES

Bloom, Benjamin S., ed., *Taxonomy of Educational Objectives.* New York: Longmans, Green & Company, Inc., 1956.

French, Will, *et al., Behavioral Goals of General Education in High School.* New York: Russell Sage Foundation, 1957.

Kearney, Nolan C., *Elementary School Objectives.* New York: Russell Sage Foundation, 1953.

TEST CONSTRUCTION

Ebel, Robert L., "Procedures for the Analysis of Classroom Tests," *Educational and Psychological Measurement,* 14 (Summer 1954), pp. 352–64.

Henry, Nelson B., ed., *The Measurement of Understanding,* Forty-Fifth Yearbook of the National Society for the Study of Education, Part I. Chicago: The University of Chicago Press, 1946.

Stodola, Quentin, *Making the Classroom Test: A Guide for Teachers,* Evaluation and Advisory Service Series, No. 4. Princeton, N.J., Educational Testing Service, 1959.

Wood, Dorothy A., *Test Construction.* Columbus, Ohio: Charles E. Merrill Company, 1960.

VALIDITY, RELIABILITY, AND NORMS

American Psychological Association, American Educational Research Association, and National Council on Measurements Used in Education, "Technical Recommendations for Psychological Tests and Diagnostic

Techniques," Supplement to the *Psychological Bulletin,* 51, Part 2, (March 1954).

Cronbach, Lee J., "Validity," in *Encyclopedia of Educational Research,* 3rd edition, ed. Chester W. Harris. New York: The Macmillan Company, 1960.

Hoyt, Cyril J., "Reliability," in *Encyclopedia of Educational Research,* 3rd edition, ed. Chester W. Harris. New York: The Macmillan Company, 1960.

Schrader, William D., "Norms," in *Encyclopedia of Educational Research,* 3rd edition, ed. Chester W. Harris. New York: The Macmillan Company, 1960.

Wert, James E., Charles O. Neidt, and J. Stanley Ahmann, *Statistical Methods in Educational and Psychological Research,* Chapters 3, 5, and 17. New York: Appleton-Century-Crofts, Inc., 1954.

APTITUDE TESTING

Harris, Chester W., "Intelligence," in *Encyclopedia of Educational Research,* 3rd edition, ed. Chester W. Harris. New York: The Macmillan Company, 1960.

Michael, William B., "Aptitudes," in *Encyclopedia of Educational Research,* 3rd edition, ed. Chester W. Harris. New York: The Macmillan Company, 1960.

Super, Donald E., and John O. Crites, *Appraising Vocational Fitness,* rev. ed. New York: Harper & Brothers, Publishers, 1962.

ACHIEVEMENT TESTING

Ebel, Robert L., and Dora E. Damrin, "Tests and Examinations," in *Encyclopedia of Educational Research,* 3rd edition, ed. Chester W. Harris. New York: The Macmillan Company, 1960.

Gerberich, J. R., *Specimen Objective Test Items.* New York: Longmans, Green & Company, Inc., 1956.

Lindquist, E. F., ed., *Educational Measurement.* Washington, D.C.: American Council on Education, 1951.

Traxler, Arthur E., *et al., Introduction to Testing and the Use of Test Results in Public Schools.* New York: Harper & Brothers, Publishers, 1953.

Index